THE LAW
AND THE LAWLESS

Frontier Justice on the Canadian Prairies, 1873–1895

EDITED BY
ART DOWNS

VICTORIA · VANCOUVER · CALGARY

Heritage House Publishing Company Ltd.
heritagehouse.ca

Library and Archives Canada Cataloguing in Publication
The law and the lawless : frontier justice on the Canadian Prairies, 1873-1895 / edited by Art Downs.

(Amazing stories)
Repackaged from: Outlaws & lawmen of Western Canada.
Issued in print and electronic formats.
ISBN 978-1-927527-86-3 (pbk.).—ISBN 978-1-927527-87-0 (html).—ISBN 978-1-927527-88-7 (pdf)

1. Outlaw—Prairie Provinces—Biography. 2. Police—Prairie Provinces—Biography. 3. Crime—Prairie Provinces—History. 4. Frontier and pioneer life—Prairie Provinces. 5. Prairie Provinces—History. I. Downs, Art, 1924-1996, editor of compilation II. Title: Frontier justice on the Canadian Prairies, 1873-1895. III. Title: Outlaws & lawmen of Western Canada. IV. Series: Amazing stories (Victoria, B.C.)

HV6805.L382 2014   364.1092'2   C2013-908573-4   C2013-908574-2

Series editor: Leslie Kenny
Proofread by Liesbeth Leatherbarrow

Cover photo: North West Mounted Police at Fort Walsh, Saskatchewan. Glenbow Archives NA-1535-1.

The interior of this book was produced on 30% post-consumer recycled paper, processed chlorine free and printed with vegetable-based inks.

Heritage House acknowledges the financial support for its publishing program from the Government of Canada through the Canada Book Fund (CBF), Canada Council for the Arts and the Province of British Columbia through the British Columbia Arts Council and the Book Publishing Tax Credit.

18 17 16 15 14   1 2 3 4 5
Printed in Canada

Contents

Publisher's Note

The stories in this collection were written several decades ago and may reflect attitudes widely held at the time that would be considered unacceptable today. Where possible, we have updated the language to more contemporary standards. In the interest of historical accuracy, material quoted from archival documents is preserved in its original form.

Prologue

THE MORNING DAWNED COOL AND *clear as Sergeant Colebrook and the police scout Francis Dumont resumed their search. Cold and tired, the two lawmen reflected on their situation. A week had passed since the escape of Almighty Voice from the jail at Duck Lake. The young Cree was known to be an impetuous if more-or-less law-abiding member of the One Arrow tribe. His crime? He had killed a stray cow to provide food for the guests at his wedding. To make matters worse, the guards on duty that night were careless and Almighty Voice had simply walked away from the jail. At most, he would face a reprimand and a few days' labour on the wood pile. A week-long search of the area had turned up nothing. Was it worth the trouble of continuing?*

Suddenly, they were startled by the near crack of a rifle. Over a slight rise they saw a Native pony beside the trail. A young girl squatted beside a fire, while a short distance away a slender young brave emerged from the trees carrying a dead rabbit.

It was Almighty Voice. Each recognized the other instantly. As Colebrook urged his horse forward, the young man dropped the rabbit and reloaded his Winchester. Colebrook continued to move forward. Almighty Voice called a warning in Cree. The officer's knowledge of Cree was slight, but Dumont translated that Almighty Voice intended to shoot. Ignoring the warning, Colebrook shifted his service revolver to his lap and lifted his hand in a sign of friendship. He was a level-headed police officer familiar with serious situations—surely the young man would not be foolish enough to shoot.

Almighty Voice raised his Winchester closer to the advancing officer and shouted again. Dumont, warned by his tone of voice, urged the policeman to stop. It was too late. Almighty Voice sent a heavy .45 caliber slug into Colebrook's chest. Stunned from the impact, he fell from his horse, the unfired revolver slipping from his fingers.

Fearing for his own life, Dumont wheeled his horse and turned back along the trail. From behind a rise, he watched while Almighty Voice approached the fallen officer and scooped up his revolver. After hurried consultation with his young bride, he mounted the officer's horse and rode eastward. The girl stoically retrieved the rabbit her husband had shot and started to cook it over the fire.

1

The March
of the Mounties

The Lawless Land

In 1869, the fledgling Dominion of Canada agreed to give the Hudson's Bay Company (HBC) some $1.5 million and land grants to relinquish its rights to Rupert's Land and its trading monopoly in what was then called the North-Western Territory. In return, the Dominion gained control of a region that would later include most of Quebec and Ontario and all of Manitoba, Saskatchewan, Alberta, Yukon, Northwest Territories, and Nunavut. A lieutenant-governor and council were appointed as administrators, and Prime Minister John A. Macdonald decided to form a mounted police force to maintain order. Unfortunately, this latter plan was dropped, and a region rivalling the US in size became a land of no law.

For some two hundred years, the HBC had administered what law there was in the West. Under its jurisdiction, chief factors were given powers to try criminal cases and endeavoured to preserve law and order for the benefit of profit and loss. Nevertheless, between 1778, when the white man first began to penetrate the plains on a regular and organized basis, and 1874, when the North West Mounted Police (NWMP) arrived, the question of crime and punishment was largely academic. Company posts were isolated, the white population small, and Native people administered their own justice.

With the transfer of the region from HBC control, a new element was introduced into the Native way of life—unlimited liquor. The HBC and other traders certainly were not teetotallers in their transactions with Native people, but they did exercise control on the sensible premise that drunken individuals made poor trappers and could be unpredictable and dangerous, let alone bad for business. Hence they strove to have the Native way of life disturbed as little as possible and even actively discouraged any settlement of their vast domain.

In the late 1860s, however, a dramatic change occurred. The American Civil War was now history, and covered wagons by the thousands rumbled across the plains carrying settlers to California, Oregon, and other western regions. Among the new communities to appear was Fort Benton on the Upper Missouri River, about 160 kilometres south of what would one day be Alberta.

Fort Benton became the supply area for a massive region

of the US plains and for unprincipled "free traders" who ventured north to challenge the HBC trading monopoly. Their main stock-in-trade was whisky. Without concern for its catastrophic consequences, they dispensed it from trading posts, or forts, as they called them, with colourful names such as Whiskey Gap, Robber's Roost, Fort Slide Out, Fort Stand Off, Spitzee Post, and Fort Whoop-Up. The latter, on the outskirts of modern-day Lethbridge and now a national historic site, became the focal point of the liquor traffic.

In 1869, John J. Healy and Alfred B. Hamilton, two US traders from Fort Benton, built eleven log cabins at the junction of the St. Mary and Oldman Rivers. They surrounded the cabins with a flimsy palisade and that winter netted $50,000. This post, called Fort Hamilton, burned down in 1871, but by that time work was well underway on a new fort a short distance away—one that wouldn't burn so easily—which became known as Fort Whoop-Up. It was built of heavy, squared timbers with a sturdy palisade loopholed for rifles and two bastions complete with cannon. On one of the bastions was a flagpole from which fluttered Healy's personal blue and red flag, which at a distance resembled the Stars and Stripes.

Native traders were seldom permitted inside the palisade. They pushed their buffalo hides and other items through a small wicket near the main gate and exchanged them for blankets, guns, and whisky—particularly whisky. Then, crazed by the firewater and thirsting for more, they often traded not only the horses they needed to hunt but also their wives and daughters.

Each trader brewed his own brutal concoction. A typical recipe diluted one gallon of raw alcohol with three gallons of water, to which was added a pound of tea, a handful of red peppers, some Jamaica ginger, a pound of chewing tobacco, some Castille soap, Perry's Painkiller, or even a dash of lye to give it "bite" since the Blackfoot liked whisky that burned on the way down. The brew was brought to a boil to blend the ingredients, then ladled out in tin cups. "I never knowed what made an Injun so crazy when he drank till I tried this booze," wrote cowboy author-artist Charles M. Russell. "You could even shoot a man through the brain or heart and he wouldn't die till he sobered up."

Probably the most damning indictment against the whisky traders was written by the Reverend John McDougall, one of the West's renowned missionaries. He noted:

Scores of thousands of buffalo robes and hundreds of thousands of wolf and fox skins and most of the best horses the Indians had were taken south into Montana, and the chief article of barter for these was alcohol. In this traffic, very many Indians were killed, and also quite a number of white men. Within a few miles of us . . . forty-two able-bodied men were the victims among themselves, all slain in the drunken rows. These were Blackfoot . . . There was no law but might. Some terrible scenes occurred when whole camps went on the spree, as was frequently the case, shooting, stabbing, killing, freezing, dying.

Missionaries and others, including the US government, the HBC, and the Canadian Pacific Railway (CPR), urged the Dominion to form a mounted force to police the West. The Dominion government responded in 1872 by sending Colonel Robertson-Ross, adjutant general for the Canadian militia, to the West for an official opinion. On his return, he promptly recommended that a mounted police force of 550 riflemen be established.

As a consequence, in May 1873, Parliament passed a bill providing for the establishment of a "Police Force in the North-West Territories," and for magistrates, courts, and jails. But Prime Minister Sir John A. Macdonald put off implementing the legislation. He didn't oppose the force—in fact he had been the primary motivator behind the legislation—but Macdonald was a marvelous procrastinator, so accomplished that he earned the nickname "Old Tomorrow."

Fortunately, Alexander Morris was among those who recognized the desperate need for a western police force. Morris had been a member of Macdonald's cabinet but resigned in 1872 to become lieutenant-governor of the province of Manitoba and the vast North-West Territories. He continued to press for a police force, cautioning Macdonald that a "most important matter . . . is the preservation of order in the Northwest and little as Canada may like it she has to stable her elephant."

But even though the legislation to establish the police

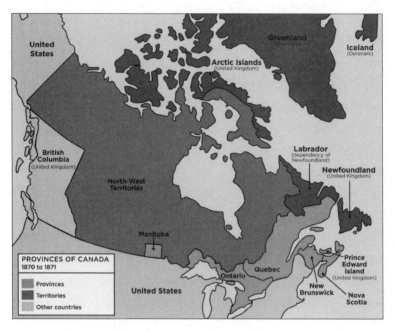

Map of Canada, 1870–71.

force had passed unanimously, Macdonald was in no hurry to "stable the elephant" and didn't intend to begin recruiting until the next year. Though he didn't know it yet, there had already been a massacre in the West that was to change his leisurely schedule.

The March of the Mounties

The Cypress Hills straddle the southern border of today's provinces of Alberta and Saskatchewan. For centuries, the area has been a favourite refuge for Native people.

Its abundant Jack pine made excellent teepee poles, and it was rich in buffalo, black and grizzly bear, deer, and other wildlife. The white men found the Cypress Hills equally attractive, especially the whisky traders. Among them were Abel Farwell and Moses Solomon, who built whisky forts nearly side by side, deep in the hills. In May 1873, a band of Assiniboine were camped near Farwell's post and, as later reported, "whiskey flowed like water . . . and by mid-day the tribesmen were all hopelessly drunk."

Probably nothing extraordinary would have happened but for the arrival of a party of wolfers—men who lived by poisoning wolves and then selling the hides. Wolfers were disliked by the Natives because their dogs were often among the poison victims. For their part, these wolfers— later described as "persons of the worst class in the country" —had no concern for either the dogs or the Native people they killed.

About noon on June 1, a man named Hammond, who was staying at Farwell's post, discovered that his horse was missing. He accused the Assiniboines and vowed to take two of their horses in retaliation. When he asked the wolfers to help, they eagerly grabbed their rifles and six-guns. It is uncertain who fired the first shot and exactly how many Assiniboine men, women, and children were killed; however, the wolfers massacred at least twenty Assiniboines, including Chief Little Soldier. He was roused from an intoxicated sleep by his wife, who attempted to lead him to the safety of the woods. He refused to go, and as he stood defenceless, he was murdered by one of the wolfers. Another old man was killed with a hatchet, his head severed, then mounted on a lodge pole. Four women were taken to Solomon's post, among them Chief Little Soldier's wife. Here, she and another young woman were repeatedly raped. The next morning the wolfers buried their only casualty, Ed Legrace, under the floor of Farwell's post, burned it and Solomon's post, then hurriedly left.

News of the slaughter was three months reaching Ottawa and even then came via US authorities. While there was indignation over the fact that "defenceless Canadian Indian women and children had been murdered by the U.S. renegades," Macdonald still held back his recruiting schedule. Then, on September 20, he received a telegram from the needling Lieutenant-Governor Morris: "What have you done as to Police Force? Their absence may lead to grave disaster."

This time the prime minister acted. On September 25, 1873, the first officers were appointed and recruiting began for 150 men. In early October, the new recruits—only two of whom had been policemen—left Ontario for Lower Fort Garry, about thirty-two kilometres north of today's Winnipeg. They travelled by lake steamer to the head of Lake Superior, then along a challenging 720-kilometre route established by fur traders. The route mostly followed rivers and lakes and included dozens of portages, some over three kilometres long. The recruits passed their first test well. When they arrived at the fur-trading post, the *Winnipeg Manitoban* reported, "Judging from the first detachment, the Mounted Police are a fine body of men."

But when the force's temporary commander, Lieutenant-Colonel W. Osborne Smith, swore in the men he must have wondered about the potential effectiveness of the "fine body of men." Most were without uniforms, arms, or other gear because everything had been frozen in between Fort Garry and Lake Superior. Worse, most of the horses were unbroken, with few of the recruits able to ride anything more vigorous than a rocking chair.

Despite these problems, training started immediately. From reveille at 6 A.M.—changed to 6:30 during the coldest winter months—until long after dark, the recruits participated in foot drill, marksmanship, riding, stable cleaning, and other duties. Sergeant Major Samuel B. Steele, destined to become the most famous of all the Mounties, was in charge of breaking the horses and teaching recruits to ride. He later wrote, "The orders were that if the temperatures were not lower than 36 below zero the riding and breaking should go on. With very few exceptions the horses were bronchos which had never been handled and . . . even when we had them 'gentled' so as to let the recruits mount, the men were repeatedly thrown with great violence to the frozen ground; but no-one lost his nerve."

On June 19, the men were sent south to Dufferin near the Manitoba–Dakota Territory border. Here they were joined by another 217 officers and men who had been recruited during the winter and trained at Toronto. Among the new contingent was Joseph Francis, a Crimean War veteran who had taken part in the famous Charge of the Light Brigade. Another was trumpeter Fred A. Bagley, at fifteen the youngest of the policemen.

By now the force had an official uniform that included a scarlet Norfolk jacket, steel-grey breeches, blue trousers with a double white stripe, and a dark blue cloak. Footwear was long black or brown boots with spurs, and the headgear was a pillbox hat or a white helmet, with matching white gauntlets. But while the uniforms were impressive, their firearms—the force's most important equipment—were not. They were issued Snider-Enfield single-shot rifles, already obsolete. Natives and whisky traders were using much superior Winchester or Henry repeating rifles. The policemen would not be issued with Winchesters for another four years.

The new force had very little information about the West. There were not over a hundred settlers in the entire region, most of them at Portage la Prairie, eighty kilometres west of Fort Garry. The only map was one made by the Palliser Expedition during an exploratory trip for the British Government in 1857–61. While it accurately showed the expedition's route, most of the map was based on information received from traders and Metis and proved remarkably unreliable.

The degree of opposition they would encounter was also

unknown. A newspaper reported that five hundred outlaws in forts and armed with repeating rifles awaited the men. Even Commissioner French expected "hot work" once they found the whisky traders. Then there were the Natives, particularly the warlike Blackfoot Nation, reportedly with two thousand warriors, who resented the white intrusion.

The force left Dufferin on July 8 with a "Hudson's Bay" start—they travelled a short distance, then camped for the night to ensure that nothing was forgotten. Under its thirty-two-year-old leader, Commissioner George A. French, the force began to march west the following day. Its primary mission, as outlined by Governor General Lord Dufferin, was "capturing a band of desperadoes who had established themselves in some fortified posts in our territory in the neighbourhood of the Belly River." Other duties included gaining the respect and confidence of the Natives and aiding settlement.

On the westward trek, Commissioner French wanted to follow a trail built by the Boundary Commission during their 1872–74 survey of the US–Canada border. There was accurate information available about the location of feed and water along this route. But the politicians, who had never seen the West, ordered otherwise—he was to follow the border some 320 kilometres only, head north, then westward. This decision forced the men to travel for weeks through a parched plain where water holes were infrequent and the livestock had to compete for grass with buffalo, grasshoppers, and prairie fires. Scores of horses and oxen died, and the men were condemned to days of unnecessary suffering. Four days after they left Dufferin, French wrote an entry in his diary he would constantly repeat: "Camped beside a marshy pool which had dried up. Got a few buckets of water by digging in mud . . . no wood or water."

To avoid the heat of the noon sun, reveille was often at 3 A.M. The cavalcade was underway an hour later, with 6 A.M. considered a late start. But the lack of feed, the heat, and the clouds of attacking mosquitoes quickly incapacitated many horses. Ten days into the march, French noted, "two horses left on road, being unfit to travel." The next day two more were left behind, and the following day two died. On July 22, French wrote, "No wood or water during morning march or afternoon march . . . I insisted on men dismounting and walking on foot every alternate hour and propose continuing this to relieve the horses."

On July 25, because of the steady weakening of the animals, Commissioner French changed his plans. His original orders were for the entire force to keep together to the foothills of the Rockies. There they would split into three groups—one remaining in the foothills, one going northward to Fort Edmonton, and the third returning to Fort Ellice. But so far they had travelled fewer than 480 kilometres of the easiest part of their estimated 1,290 kilometres, and it was obvious that many—if not most—of the animals would die. French countermanded orders by sending "A" Division northward to Fort Ellice where a fur-traders' cart trail led to Fort Edmonton.

Inspector W.D. Jarvis left on July 29 with Sergeant Major Sam Steele on the 1,450-kilometre trek to Fort Edmonton. With them went twenty-four wagons, fifty-five carts, twenty men, and the weakest of the livestock. They reached Fort Edmonton on October 27 after a dreadful journey that included continuing problems with the weak animals and, in contrast with what the main body of troops experienced, too much water. Steele later wrote, "The trail was worse than any we had encountered. It was knee-deep in black mud, sloughs crossed it every hundred yards, and the wagons had to be unloaded and dragged through them by hand."

While Jarvis and his group battled toward Fort Edmonton, Commissioner French and the remainder of the main force trudged westward. They reached the Boundary Commission's post at Wood Depot the same day that Jarvis left. Here they remained all day "to allow men to cook and bake 3 days rations, and secure a supply of wood for 3 more days, as it is doubtful whether we will be able to get wood for a week." Four days later French observed that there was no wood, stating, "Those Troops that did not carry enough wood on their waggons are now beginning to feel the effects of their thoughtlessness."

On August 4, a fierce storm created additional discomfort. Tents were blown away, and two men became lost. "Had a gun and rocket fired," French wrote. "They both, fortunately, turned up all right to-day, being pretty well frightened at the idea of being so easily lost on the prairie." The seeming endlessness of the prairie impressed not only the two men who were lost. Among those on the trip was Henri Julien, staff artist for the *Canadian Illustrated News*, who wrote:

> The prairies over which we travelled presented the same undulating, monotonous appearance. Not one green bush of the most dwarfish size to relieve the eye . . . The eye dwells on vacancy, tired of glancing at the blue sky above or the brown earth beneath. A feeling of weariness creeps over you, interrupted at intervals by vague longings for something beyond the far low line of the horizon, which is ever barred across your vision. The silence is oppressing . . . This has truly been called "The Great Lone Land."

By then, French had realized that his guides were unreliable. He kept a check on directions and distance with a prismatic compass and an odometer. "Had a long pow-wow with guides," noted one diary entry. "Found that one of them was a regular imposter."

The Mounties received their first visit from the Sioux on August 12. French wrote, "It appears there has been a fight near the Cypress Hills . . . The half-breed and Sioux appear to have killed all the Black-feet." The next day there was a formal meeting where French was given the name "Wachasta Sota," or "Man with Power," and the Sioux entertained the policemen with "dance and song."

On August 19, French decided to leave the sickest men and weakest animals behind until they returned on the homeward journey. At this aptly named "Cripple Camp," he left Constable Sutherland and seven men, twelve wagons, and twenty-six sick and weak horses. Continuing on, they saw their first buffalo on September 2 and killed five, but while the buffalo provided meat for the men, they also consumed forage needed for the horses and fouled the scarce water sources.

Adding to their problems were the two nine-pound cannons. As Julien noted: "Our two pieces of artillery were the most difficult of all to manage, weighing 4,400 lbs. They were always in the way, retarded our march, took up the time of several men and the service of several good horses. They were not fired off even once at an enemy, and, in fact, had hostilities been encountered, would have been of less use than the rifles which the gunners should have carried."

On September 6, French had more problems when his guide insisted that they had reached the Bow River, their preliminary destination. "I told him we were at least 70 miles from the Bow," French wrote. "We have in fact reached the South Saskatchewan . . . The Scout has brought us nearly a day's march out of our road during the last two days . . . I am not quite sure whether his actions are due to ignorance or design. He is the greatest liar I have ever met. He is suspected as being a spy for the [Fort] Whoop up villains, but there is nothing definite or tangible to show this."

Two days later, the weather changed to cold rain with heavy wind. The next day five horses died, "paralyzed with cold and hunger," and the following day, two more. To protect the animals, French had each officer and man donate one of his blankets to cover the horses. In addition, everyone was now walking much of the time to spare the horses.

Fortunately, the weather improved, unlike the year before when a three-day September blizzard swept the area, killing animals and men. On September 12, they reached the junction of the Belly and Bow Rivers, the supposed location of the whisky traders' Fort Whoop-Up. There was neither fort nor traders ready for battle. Instead, French wrote, "The Fort!!! at the Forks of the Bow and Belly Rivers turns out to be three log huts without roofs in which some fellows occasionally stopped when trapping or rather poisoning wolves." French would have been even more upset had he known that the fort was some 130 kilometres away and that the policemen would be another month reaching it.

On September 13 and 14, another nine horses died from cold and hunger. French decided to head south to the Sweet Grass Hills where, the guides assured him, grass and water were plentiful. This time the guides were correct, and on September 18 the force camped in a coulee not far from the Montana border. The day before, four more horses had dropped, while all the oxen had to be abandoned since they were too weak to travel. The men were little better, being exhausted by the long hours of pushing wagons and suffering from poor water and food that consisted mostly of buffalo, flour, and dried potatoes. Their once-red tunics were dirty and torn, and many whose boots had worn out wore sacks on their feet.

After resting a few days, French, Assistant Commissioner James F. Macleod, and eight others left for Fort Benton on the Upper Missouri River, some 160 kilometres to the south. Free of the wagons and cumbersome cannon, they made fast progress. On the third day, after crossing the Maria and Teton Rivers eleven times, they rode into Fort Benton at noon. There, French purchased moccasins, boots, gloves, and stockings for his men, and corn and oats for the horses. He was surprised to find that the merchants were friendly, since many of them were deeply involved in the whisky trade and should have resented the arrival of the police. Isaac Baker, who had financed construction of Fort Whoop-Up for his nephew, Alfred B. Hamilton, was especially co-operative. He not only told French the location of the elusive fort but described the good wagon trail leading to it from Benton. He also introduced him to Jerry Potts, a half-Scottish, half-Blood guide.

French hired Potts for $90 a month, a move that would be immensely beneficial to the force. The NWMP now had a guide who proved to be a plainsman without parallel and would loyally serve until his death twenty-two years later. Sam Steele would summarize Jerry's guiding ability in these words: "As scout and guide I have never met his equal, he had none in either the North West or the States to the south."

Jerry was the son of Andrew Potts, a Scot employed by the American Fur Company, and a Blood woman. While Jerry was still a baby, his father was murdered by a Peigan. For the next few years, he was cared for by Alexander Harvey, a man whose contempt for Natives was typical of most plainsmen. In the early 1840s, because his employee had been murdered, Harvey fired a cannon into a group of unsuspecting Blackfoot, killing thirteen. Whether or not the Blackfoot were guilty was of no interest to Harvey. As far as he was concerned, the deaths were a just revenge.

Fortunately for Potts, irate citizens forcefully urged Harvey to settle elsewhere. Potts was then cared for by Andrew Dawson, who not only taught Jerry to speak English and five Native dialects, but instilled in him an understanding and pride for both his white and Native heritage. Jerry also became a superb horseman and a crack shot with a six-gun or rifle.

For his first assignment for the Mounties, Potts guided French back to the Sweet Grass Hills. In compliance with his orders, French handed command over to Macleod and left to rejoin "D" and "E" Troops, which had already begun the 1,290-kilometre trek to a new headquarters near Fort Pelly. Macleod and the rest of the force turned northwest toward Fort Whoop-Up.

When the force finally reached Fort Whoop-Up on

October 9, Macleod anticipated a fight and deployed his cannons, despite Jerry's assessment that the whisky peddlers had fled. The only movement at the fort was the trader's flag fluttering above the bastion. With Potts at his side, Macleod rode straight toward the fort with his men, who were every second expecting rifles to blast from the loopholed palisade. Then Macleod halted, dismounted, and strode through the wide-open gate. He entered the silent fort and knocked on the door of the nearest building. A bearded, grey-haired trader named Dave Akers opened it and invited the police "to come right in." He was the only white occupant. As Potts had predicted, the whisky traders had left with their liquor when they learned about the approaching police.

Macleod offered to buy Whoop-Up as headquarters for $10,000, but Akers wanted $25,000. Since Macleod didn't have this much money, he decided to build his own post. Potts led them some fifty kilometres to the northwest to an island in the Oldman River. Here was plenty of grass, water, and timber to build a fort. Work started immediately on the first NWMP post in the West, named Fort Macleod on orders from Commissioner French.

The storied Fort Whoop-Up didn't have long to survive. Akers continued trading—but not whisky—and raising prize-winning cabbages in the compound. In 1888, fire destroyed much of the fort, and in 1894 Akers was shot dead by his former partner, Tom Purcell. Unfortunately for Purcell, the lawless era was history. He was promptly arrested by the Mounties but on pleading self-defence was given a jail sentence instead of being hanged.

Purcell was only one of scores who experienced the consequences of the new era of law and order. Even while the policemen were living in tents and rushing to complete Fort Macleod before the onset of blizzards and sub-zero temperatures, patrols searched for whisky traders. On October 30, only a few days after they arrived, Colonel Macleod reported to Commissioner French that we have "struck a first blow at the liquor traffic in this country."

Macleod had learned from a Native man named Three Bulls that a half-black, half-Mexican man, William Bond, had a whisky post at Pine Coulee some eighty kilometres from Fort Macleod. Bond had traded Three Bulls nine litres of whisky for two horses. It was a satisfactory transaction for Bond, since horses were worth some $200 each, the whisky perhaps one-twentieth that amount. Three Bulls felt he had been short-changed and decided to test the fairness of the red-coated horsemen.

As a result, a patrol under Inspector L.N. Crozier arrested Bond and four others. The policemen confiscated two wagons containing cases of alcohol, 16 horses, 5 Henry rifles, 5 revolvers, and 116 buffalo robes, which became warm clothing for the ill-clad policemen. All those involved were fined, a sentence that led to the identification of a leading figure in the whisky trade. J.B. Weatherwax was a prominent Montana businessman with contempt for anything resembling law and order. He paid the fines of all except Bond, who was kept at the police post to serve his sentence. As yet, the policemen were too busy building shelters for their animals and themselves—the stables were built before the barracks—to spend time constructing a jail. As a result, on December 2, Bond escaped while being taken from one building to another. As he sprinted away, one of the guards fired, but Bond escaped. Under the harsh discipline of the force, those responsible for guarding Bond were sentenced to jail, although the whisky trader paid heavily for being the first man to escape custody. The next spring, his body was found a few kilometres from the fort, a bullet between his shoulders. By now, Colonel Macleod had learned that Bond was wanted for murder in Ontario and had also deliberately killed a Blackfoot man. It is not known for certain who killed Bond, although the bullet fired by the guard was probably the cause.

As a result of arresting Bond and the other traders, the police learned the location of two more whisky forts. In February, despite blizzards and below-zero weather, nine men under Inspector Crozier, with Jerry Potts as guide, left Fort Macleod to arrest the traders. Their destination was about 160 kilometres to the northwest, but because of blizzards and cold they were eighteen days on the trek. On one occasion, several policemen lost the trail during a storm but were found by Potts, even though visibility was less than thirty metres.

NWMP artillery detachment at Fort Macleod, 1890s.
GLENBOW ARCHIVE NA-2646-1

Among those arrested during the frigid trek were several of Weatherwax's men. Weatherwax himself was rounded up by another midwinter patrol of five policemen led by Sub-Inspector Cecil E. Denny. Denny and two policemen surprised Weatherwax and two other men drinking and playing cards in a big log house. The policemen found a large stock of liquor and hundreds of furs and robes. The men were arrested and taken to Fort Macleod on a trip that took three days. Here they were fined $250 by Macleod, and their teams, robes, and other possessions were confiscated.

Weatherwax was a tall, imposing man. Denny noted he was "most defiant, threatening dire consequences to follow an appeal he should make to Washington. He failed to impress Colonel Macleod, who told him to pay his fine or go to jail, and so far as an appeal to Washington was concerned he was welcome to go the limit. He spent a week in the guardroom; then as hard labour was the lot of all prisoners—wood-cutting, stable-cleaning, and other jobs—he paid his fine and was released."

When news of Weatherwax's arrest and sentence reached Fort Benton, the local newspaper indignantly noted, "Wherever the British flag floats, might is right, but we had no idea that the persons and property of American citizens would be trifled with in the manner that American merchants have been." It went on to suggest that American troops march north so that "the Bull-dogs would be properly chained and controlled." Since the newspaper was owned by J.J. Healy, one of the men who had skinned the Natives at Fort Whoop-Up, the criticism was understandable. But Healy and Weatherwax had already learned something that would be proved over and over—the Mounted Police didn't scare worth a cent. Some of them, however, died while helping to build this reputation.

The first member to die in the West was Constable Godfrey Parks. He died of typhoid on October 26, and became the first occupant of a cemetery established between Fort Macleod and the river. Just over two months later, he was joined by two others. On December 30, Constables Baxter and Wilson left Fort Macleod for Fort Kipp, but were caught in a sudden storm. When their riderless horses reached Fort Kipp, a search was started by Blackfoot trackers. They soon found Baxter's lifeless body, then Wilson. He was alive but died shortly after.

Despite these tragedies, the force continued its pressure on the whisky peddlers. By the spring of 1875, the trade had declined abruptly from a flourishing enterprise to a minor nuisance. Without a shot, the policemen had swiftly accomplished their primary mission and built their outpost of Fort Macleod at the same time. The lawmen were equally successful in their second objective—winning the friendship of the Natives. When the Blackfoot Nation gathered in 1877 to sign Treaty 6, Crowfoot, their legendary chief, summarized his people's feelings:

> If the Police had not come to the country, where would we all be now? Bad men and whiskey were killing us so fast that very few, indeed, of us would have been left to-day. The Police have protected us as the feathers of the bird protect it from the frosts of winter. I wish them all good, and trust that all our hearts will increase in goodness from this time forward. I am satisfied. I will sign the treaty.

Perhaps the biggest challenge to peace began in 1876 when the warlike Sioux retreated into Canada after slaughtering Lieutenant Colonel George A. Custer and his entire 7th Cavalry at the Battle of the Little Bighorn. Eventually there were some six thousand Sioux in the Cypress Hills under Chief Sitting Bull, with only a few redcoats under Superintendent J.M. Walsh to oversee them. Despite serious food shortages and other tensions, Walsh befriended Sitting Bull and shared food from NWMP rations. To

Walsh's credit, peace was maintained, and by 1881 almost all of the Sioux had returned to the US.

During the Riel Rebellion, many Mounties served with distinction, among them Sam Steele, who commanded a group of cowboys, settlers, and policemen called Steele's Scouts. Among those who died fighting the rebels was John French, Commissioner George A. French's brother, who had resigned from the force in 1883 and was an officer in the militia. But so little did Ottawa bureaucrats and politicians appreciate the efforts of the policemen that while all citizen-soldiers received medals within one year, those men who had been scouts and were usually the first to be shot at weren't awarded medals for three years.

The delayed campaign ribbon wasn't the only example of shabby treatment. In 1879, the policemen's pay was virtually halved, with a sub-constable's reduced from seventy-five cents a day to forty cents. It did not return to seventy-five cents for over a quarter-century. As a further insult, the free grant of sixty-five hectares at the end of a satisfactory enlistment was cancelled. In 1883 at Fort Macleod the men staged a revolt to protest the conditions. For months they had been fed bread, beef, and tea three times a day, the meat frequently fit only for garbage. Uniforms were not replaced, and on their cut-rate wages the men had to borrow money and pay interest to feed and clothe themselves. The men all bought Stetson cowboy hats, since the pillbox type was useless for Western weather. The pillboxes weren't officially replaced until about 1900, or twenty-five years after they were issued.

Yet despite the poor treatment they received, the men worked faithfully to uphold the motto of the force, "Maintain the Right." In the years that followed the Riel Rebellion, the Mounties completed the third of their initial objectives—overseeing the peaceful settlement by hundreds of thousands of people on the Western plains. One of their duties in the 1890s was the protection of tens of thousands of prairie settlers, most of whom had never been out of the city. The hazards of prairie life included fires that swept the plains with the speed of a galloping horse, blizzards that made venturing from house to barn perilous, injury, illness, and a host of other potentially disastrous situations. To help safeguard them, every inhabitant was listed and regular patrols started, each settler signing a patrol sheet when a Mountie checked. The area covered by horseback and by buggy was awesome. In one year alone, patrols out of Regina travelled nearly 563,000 kilometres, a distance equivalent to four times around the world with a side trip to the moon.

In his December 1874 report, the NWMP's first commissioner, George A. French, summarized his feelings toward the men he had commanded on the march: "A Canadian force, hastily raised, armed, and equipped, and not under martial law, in a few months marched 2,000 miles, through a country for the most part as unknown as it proved bare of pasture and scanty in the supply of water. Of such a march, under such circumstances, all true Canadians may well feel proud."

2

The Death of Manitoba's First Police Chief

THE MANITOBA PROVINCIAL POLICE (MPP) was formed in October 1870, shortly after the province's entry into Canada. Under the leadership of Captain John Villiers, assisted by Louis de Plainval, nineteen men were sworn in, issued with a miscellany of weapons and nondescript uniforms, and posted throughout the thinly populated region. Nineteen-year-old Richard Power was one of the original members.

Within two years, few originals remained. While most of the men resigned to accept positions in the rapidly expanding business world of Winnipeg, one was dismissed for drunkenness and striking his superior officer, and another received a five-year sentence for the shooting death of a young soldier at Fort Garry barracks. Even Richard Power narrowly escaped dismissal for shooting a Native during an arrest.

As officers resigned or were dismissed, they were not replaced, and the force shrank from nineteen to a pathetic eight-man squad. Partly as a result of this rapid depletion, but more because of his ability for police work, Power was promoted rapidly until February 1874 when he was appointed chief constable at the age of twenty-three.

Just before his appointment, Winnipeg had incorporated as a city and created its own small police force under John S. Ingram. Power, now responsible for policing the rest of the province, revamped his force by stationing men at posts such as Selkirk, Kildonan, and St. Norbert—outside Winnipeg but where the population was concentrated. His headquarters were in a log building just off Winnipeg's Main Street and here he stationed the remainder of his small force. Law enforcement at places like Portage la Prairie and Emerson had to depend on vigilantes and volunteer police.

Across the Canadian-American border in neighbouring Dakota Territory, law enforcement officers numbered even fewer. There was only one officer, Sheriff Brown, at Pembina, with the nearest help some distance away at Fargo. As a consequence, so long as outlaws stayed away from the few populated centres, they could operate with impunity.

View of Winnipeg, 1874. MANITOBA ARCHIVES N143

Among these outlaws was Edward Couture, who headed a gang from a hideout south of Pembina. Their method was to make quick midnight horse raids on the farms of Manitoba settlers and scamper back before the MPP arrived. The stolen horses were then driven deep into Dakota Territory and sold.

Chief Constable Power's involvement with the gang was the result of a telegram from F.T. Bradley, customs officer and Justice of the Peace at the border village of Emerson. He advised that one of Couture's gang, Edward Martin, was heading north to visit relatives. As dawn broke over Winnipeg on September 7, 1874, Power and a constable named Heusens saddled up and rode south along the stagecoach road to the twin border villages of Emerson and Pembina. Subsequent events were an indication of Power's courage, tenacity, and luck, since he should have died during his first encounter with Martin. The events also demonstrated that Martin could break from prison as easily as he stole a horse.

It was a seventy-kilometre ride from Winnipeg to the stagecoach station at Scratching River (Morris), where Power planned to lie in wait for the horse thief. Darkness had fallen when the lawmen arrived within sight of the stopping place. They left their horses with a nearby settler and approached on foot. Moments later two horsemen rode in from the south. It was Edward Martin and a fellow outlaw, Charles Garden. Power noted that the horse Martin was riding resembled the description of one stolen the previous month. He stepped forward and seized the bridle. At the same time, Heusens grasped Garden by the pant leg. Ordered to dismount, the two men got down quietly.

As it was too dark to return to Winnipeg, Power decided to keep his prisoners, who were not considered dangerous, at the stagecoach station for the night and start early the following morning. He walked Martin forward while Heusens remained with Garden to care for the horses. As they passed through the entrance to the station, Martin lunged at Power, throwing him off balance. Before the officer could recover, Martin drew a revolver and fired at point-blank range. His first shot missed. As he swung round for a second, Power recovered his balance and grappled with him in the room.

Heusens and Garden, hearing the shot, started for the station—but with different intentions. Heeding a shout from Martin, Garden sprang into the room and swept a coal-oil lamp from the table, plunging the room into darkness. He then drew a hunting knife from his boot and flung himself on Constable Heusens. That was a mistake. Heusens stood door-high and was a hefty mass of muscle and bone. With a sweep of his hand he bounced Garden off the nearest wall and leaped to Power's assistance. Meanwhile, Martin had managed to get his finger on the trigger and fired a couple of random shots. Garden did not appreciate the flying bullets and scrambled for the door.

Power broke loose from Martin, pulled his Colt .45—the largest model made with a nine-inch barrel—and ordered Martin to drop his gun. The outlaw complied meekly. Leaving Heusens to guard him, Power started in pursuit of Garden. A noise sent him in the direction of the corral where he glimpsed a figure sprinting into the darkness. Power fired and heard a muffled cry, but it was too dark to investigate and he returned to the station.

The following morning, Power found traces of blood near the corral and realized that he had hit Garden. Ordering Heusens to escort Martin to the prison in Winnipeg, he saddled his horse and began tracking the escapee. His job was made easier when a settler brought word that Garden was in his shack with a leg wound, seeking refuge. Power quickly arrested him and with a borrowed team and wagon took him to Winnipeg. Here he was given medical attention and jailed—but only for a short time.

At 11 P.M. on October 1, Constable Heusens made the rounds of the prison. He checked each prisoner through a peephole in the cell door, noted that all was in order and went back to the office. Heusens was relieved at midnight by another constable. On making his inspection, he noticed that prisoner Charles Bigeral's cell door was not closed tight and that the "figure" lying on the bunk was a dummy. A quick check of other cell doors revealed that all were locked except Edward Martin's, whose bunk also contained a roll of blankets made to look like a sleeping man. Garden, Martin's partner, still slumbered peacefully in his cell.

Undetected, Martin and Bigeral had picked five locks from the cell door to the corridor, then proceeded to the central square where they had opened and relocked doors leading to the centre hall. Here, without being seen, they picked the massive lock on the main door and walked into the street.

There was no telephone in the prison and the solitary guard spent considerable time finding someone to alert Chief Constable Power. It was nearly morning before a pursuit was organized. Power suspected that a gang member named Rogers was an accomplice since he had been seen in the vicinity of the prison on several occasions following Martin's arrest. He also believed—correctly as events proved—that Rogers had met the escapees outside the prison with horses and a change of clothing.

After meeting Rogers, the fugitives rode south across the border where Bigeral parted from Martin and Rogers. Freedom for the latter two was short, however. In response to telegraphic warnings by Power to sheriffs in Dakota and Minnesota, they were captured near Glyndon, Minnesota, on October 23. With them were five stolen horses.

Martin was jailed at Moorhead, North Dakota, to await trial for possession of stolen property and possible extradition to Manitoba. The warden, aware of his ability to pick locks, placed him in leg irons and added a second lock to the cell door. Martin bided his time. On May 5, 1875, Martin picked both locks, then released his leg irons with a key from the sheriff's office. There were too many people on the street to risk walking out, so he bored a hole through the side wall of the office and let himself into the space between the jail and an adjacent building.

Martin was next reported at Cheyenne, where he stole a boat and headed for the Canadian border. A few days later he was captured at Sioux Falls with two stolen horses. He was taken to Fargo under heavy guard and sentenced to serve a severe term in the territorial prison, from which he did not escape. On release he was believed to have headed west for the more hospitable climes of Montana Territory.

The remainder of the horse thieves were rounded up by Power and the MPP or by Dakota authorities. The leader,

Edward Couture, was brought to trial in Winnipeg on June 14, 1875. He was charged with sixteen counts of horse theft, but his lawyers managed to get a four-month postponement. Couture never came to trial since he also escaped from the Winnipeg prison and headed south, although his arrest did break up the gang.

But tracking horse thieves and chasing prison escapees were only part of Chief Constable Power's duties. He was also involved in several murder cases. His first major case was that of Joseph Michaud, who was hanged in public in 1874 for murdering James R. Brown. Then followed the conviction of Gilbert Godon for slaying Benjamin Marchand.

In 1875, Power was confronted with two murders. On May 3, the body of John O'Maley was discovered in a small stream near the border. The motive apparently was $1,000 O'Maley had in his possession. Two weeks later, Power was presented with a second body from the same river. Like O'Maley, the man had been shot several times, wrapped in heavy chains, and dumped in the river. Despite a thorough investigation of the twin murders, no one was ever brought to trial.

Power was more successful in the spring of 1878 when he and a posse captured killer John Gribbon. Gribbon was convicted of manslaughter but he, too, escaped from jail and crossed into the US. He was later arrested by American authorities, then released in November 1879 on a legal technicality. He was re-arrested the following day at the urging of Chief Power for the suspected murders of two women several years before, but he was again set free when Power was not given time to prepare a strong enough case.

A few months later, Power was involved with another prison escapee—Edward Daniels. This encounter nearly proved fatal for Power. The case of Edward Daniels began on June 16, 1875, when he was sentenced to two years for stealing from a Winnipeg store. His prison stay also was brief. On the afternoon of September 18, a small group of men, including Daniels, were working in the prison yard under the surveillance of a solitary guard. One prisoner on the roof called for instructions. The guard shouted back, but the inmate protested that he did not understand, forcing the guard to climb the ladder. When the guard returned, Daniels was missing.

It was later learned from Daniels's diary that the night after his escape he burgled the home of Captain Kennedy, a Justice of the Peace for whom he had once worked. He helped himself to provisions and clothing before making his way to Winnipeg, where he stole a horse and buggy and travelled by back roads across the border into Dakota. His first stop was Deadwood, where he used the name William Chiraton and posed as a freighter from Manitoba. At that time, Deadwood was a hangout for notorious gamblers such as Wild Bill Hickok, as well as gunmen, whisky traders, and gold seekers. Daniels recorded in his diary that twice he was involved in gunfights but managed to escape both times. Since the diary was for Daniels's own use, it is unlikely that he invented these incidents.

The following autumn, still using the name Chiraton, he returned to Manitoba, again burgling Captain Kennedy's home. He outfitted himself with food and clothing, then burgled several other homes in the area before moving east. He went into hiding by hiring on as a construction worker on the CPR.

But Winnipeg seemed to fascinate him, and in October 1876 he was back. This time, however, he spared the unfortunate Captain Kennedy by stealing a horse from a Mr. Campbell. He hid the animal in the woods and returned, but this time was seen boldly leading a horse from Reverend Matheson's stable. Daniels managed to escape before the police arrived.

Chief Constable Richard Power doggedly followed his man from farm to farm along the stagecoach road to Emerson. He found Campbell's horse at a settler's farm and was told that Daniels had also sold a horse to the settler the previous year. Power inspected the animal and confirmed that it was one stolen from a resident of St. Andrews.

Learning that his man was only a few hours ahead, Power telegraphed Sheriff Brown at Pembina. Daniels was apprehended on October 25 as he rode into town on Reverend Matheson's horse. As a consequence, in June 1877, Edward Daniels was convicted of bringing stolen property into Dakota and sentenced to two years in Stillwater Territorial

Penitentiary, largely on evidence provided by Power. The outlaw and the lawman, however, were not yet free of each other.

Daniels was released in 1879 and returned to Manitoba and his old way of life. Prison had made him more bitter and dangerous, as was evident when he burgled the house of a Mrs. Ross. When she surprised him in the act, Daniels showed her he was well armed and said he would kill the first man who tried to arrest him. As soon as her unwelcome visitor left, she hastened to Captain Kennedy who instructed MPP detectives Smith and Macdonald to bring in the outlaw, dead or alive.

Learning that Daniels was heading for St. Boniface, the two detectives went to a saloon owned by Louis Platcher, one of many who sympathized with Daniels. Although Daniels was warned that the detectives were waiting, he could not resist baiting them. Two nights later he walked into the saloon disguised in a woman's cloak and, as later learned, two revolvers thrust into his belt. After purchasing a bottle of whisky within a few feet of the detectives, he sauntered casually through the front entrance.

Despite the disguise, however, Daniels had been recognized by several people in the saloon. But they feared warning the detectives while he was still inside in case a shootout resulted. Once alerted, Smith and Macdonald gave chase, but Daniels eluded them in the dark. It was then he dropped his diary, which recorded his adventures and crimes since escaping from the penitentiary in 1875.

Daniels crossed the border to Pembina, where he joined a band of horse thieves. But within three months he was back in the Winnipeg area. For some strange reason, he seemed to take pleasure in stealing from the same people. Reverend Matheson's stable was revisited and the same horse stolen again. He next went to Mary Inkster's home, where he helped himself to seven bottles of beer, despite the protests of that astonished lady.

In response to Mrs. Inkster's call for help, a posse of six men assembled in her yard. They were still debating a judicious course of action when Chief Constable Power rode up with Special Constable Sam Gerrard. Under Power's direction the posse scoured the area.

The search continued through the night without success. Then at 10 A.M. the following day, Power received a surprising message. The young criminal was at a farmstead, cutting the grass. But the driveway to the place offered no concealment and Daniels easily recognized the approaching Power. In seconds he was headed for the nearest woods astride the unfortunate Matheson horse.

Instead of chasing Daniels, Power changed tactics. He left the Kildonan area, stating that he had received word that Daniels was in another part of the province. He counted on this message being relayed to Daniels and hoped that the outlaw's daring and bravado would lead him into an error of judgment. Power was not disappointed.

Early Wednesday morning, two men brought word that

Daniels was staying the night with a friend in St. Paul's. Stationing Gerrard outside the bedroom window, Power entered the house and carefully eased open the bedroom door. Despite Power's stealth and caution, Daniels was alert. As Power stepped into the room, gun drawn, the outlaw raised his revolver and pulled the trigger. There was a click but no flash of flame. The gun had misfired, saving Power from almost certain death. Daniels hurled the useless weapon aside and dived for a second revolver on the bed. With incredible fortitude, Chief Constable Power refrained from shooting the trapped man. As Daniels whirled with the second gun in hand, he found himself looking down the muzzle of Power's massive .45. He dropped his revolver and backed away.

Handcuffed and shackled, Daniels was taken to the provincial jail at Winnipeg. Despite the fact that he was well known to Power, he said that his name was Frank Morris and that he had never heard of Edward Daniels. He maintained this subterfuge even when his aunt identified him. Only when the penitentiary warden advised him to admit his identity, return to the penitentiary, and complete as much as possible of his original sentence before new ones were imposed did Daniels relent.

Two months later, Edward Daniels was brought before Chief Justice Wood and charged with a handful of offences dating back to the first theft of Reverend Matheson's horse in 1876. Convicted of some crimes and acquitted of others for lack of evidence, he received sentences totalling fourteen years. Had his revolver not misfired, he could well have killed Power and been sentenced to hang.

Although Power escaped death while capturing both Daniels and Martin, he was not so fortunate in his next encounter with a fugitive. Mike Carroll was one of those frontier types known as a "hard case." He drifted into the Fort William area of Ontario in the mid-1880s, seeking employment on the CPR being built to Rat Portage (Kenora). His real talent, however, lay in picking pockets rather than driving spikes, with fellow workmen quickly relieved of their wallets.

Arrested for these relatively slight misdemeanours, Carroll was given a short sentence in the lockup at Rat Portage. Then authorities discovered that he had a long record in eastern Canada that included an escape from Toronto's Central Prison, considered to have the ultimate in security measures. Carroll was also credited with several other prison breaks and soon added Rat Portage's jail to his list.

Unfortunately for Carroll, he tended to be talkative. As a result, word soon reached Detective O'Keefe of the MPP that his man was at Selkirk, north of Winnipeg. He wired Detective Malcolm McKenzie at Cross Lake, who caught the first train to Selkirk. Tracking his man to the hotel dining room, McKenzie invited him to hold out his wrists for handcuffs. Instead, Carroll shoved a table into McKenzie's stomach and darted through the door. Like most Manitoba

The jail at Rat Portage near Kenora, 1883.
LAKE OF THE WOODS MUSEUM

policemen, McKenzie had been selected for size rather than for speed, and the ensuing foot race was no contest. The frustrated detective sent several bullets after the fleet little outlaw, but Carroll escaped into the darkness.

Fortunately for the police, Carroll still hadn't learned the value of silence. He could not resist bragging about his escapade to a barber who passed the information to Power. The outlaw quickly found himself back in jail. This time he evidently had realized the value of silence, for he remained quiet until Detective O'Keefe told him he planned to return him to Ontario to face prison-breaking and other charges. If this transfer happened, Carroll threatened, he would drown the detective while crossing Lake of the Woods, even if he perished himself.

Despite the threat, on July 3, 1880, Carroll was escorted by Power and McKenzie to Rat Portage. Here he was found guilty by Magistrate C.J. Brereton and sentenced to two years. At that time, the territory around Rat Portage was a political wilderness, with magistrates having the option of sentencing prisoners to serve time either in Manitoba or Ontario. In Carroll's case, Brereton decided that Winnipeg's prison offered better security than the Rat Portage lockup— especially in view of the man's history of escapes. He therefore ordered Detective O'Keefe to transport Carroll back to Manitoba.

Despite Carroll's threat to drown O'Keefe, the journey was accomplished successfully and he was jailed on July 8. But not for long. On July 23, Carroll was one of a group of prisoners cutting wood at the government offices on Main Street. The guard in charge had taken the precaution of asking for a ball and chain for Carroll, but this request was denied. Later that day, a man in prison clothing was reported sprinting along Main Street in the direction of a bridge being built across the Red River between Winnipeg and St. Boniface.

Chief Constable Power was in bed with fever when advised of Carroll's escape. He dressed, strapped on his Colt .45, and collected Constable J. Bell. Together they traced the escapee to the bridge that he had crossed in full view of the workmen. From there, trailing the escapee was simple since Carroll had escaped minus his shoes, a safety precaution on guard McKay's part. Several people had noticed a man carefully picking his way along the railway track south of St. Boniface.

The search ended at a haystack late that evening. Carroll, his feet cut and swollen, emerged and simply grinned in resignation when he saw the two policemen. Power commandeered a railway handcar and, with all three taking turns, they pumped themselves back to St. Boniface. They arrived at the village about midnight to find the ferry not running. However, a man with a rowboat offered to take them across. Power stepped into the boat first and turned to help his handcuffed prisoner. By accident or design, Carroll put his foot on the gunwale, and the boat overturned. Both men disappeared beneath the surface of the river.

In the darkness, Bell and the boatman caught a glimpse of Carroll a few lengths downstream, but Richard Power was never seen alive again. His body was found the next morning not far from the loading dock, weighed down by the ammunition belt and heavy Colt .45. Carroll's body was discovered some distance downstream. His earlier threat to drown O'Keefe led to speculation that the outlaw had deliberately upset the rowboat in order to escape.

The *Manitoba Daily Free Press* carried a full account of the tragedy in its July 28, 1880, edition, noting:

The city was surprised and grieved this morning by the announcement that Richard Power, Chief of the Provincial Police, had been drowned during the night while attempting to cross the Red River with a prisoner—the notorious Mike Carroll. It seemed impossible to realize the fact that he, who was in our midst but yesterday in the prime of his vigor and manhood, had been thus suddenly cut off, even while in the active discharge of his duties.

An editorial in the same edition noted:

By the untimely death of Mr. Richard Power . . . the Province loses, we believe, its oldest, and we are sure one of its most faithful and efficient officers. Mr. Power entered the public service at the very organization of the Province in the capacity of a mounted policeman, and has ever since been connected with the police, for the most of the time as chief. Fear was a quality which Mr. Power, it is said by those who knew him best, did not possess. His deeds of daring and intrepidity are numerous, and it was the prognostication of his acquaintances that he would certainly die on duty.

Constable Power was buried with full military honours, including a gun carriage to carry his body to the cemetery. During his funeral, activity in the community virtually halted. As the newspaper noted, "His friends are numbered by hundreds."

CHAPTER

3

Alberta Cannibal: Swift Runner

THE PROBLEM OF DISPOSING OF the victim's body has plagued murderers since the days of Cain. Burial, burning, dismemberment, acid, and quicklime have been tried, but with no statistics it is impossible to determine whether one method is more effective than another. By and large, however, murderers tend to leave their victims where they fall, or at best make only a casual effort to conceal their crime. One exception was a Cree man named Swift Runner, notable primarily for the method he used to dispose of most of the evidence.

Swift Runner, or Kak-say-kwyo-chin, was a quiet, thoughtful man. For hours at a time he would sit immobile, a look of utter satisfaction on his face, staring into space. But beneath

53

his calm exterior there lurked the fires and tortures of an old-fashioned Hell, for at night Swift Runner was a troubled man. Again and again he would waken from his sleep, moaning that the Native spirit of evil, Ween-de-go, was plaguing him with horrible dreams.

Swift Runner had appeared dramatically at the little Roman Catholic mission at St. Albert, just north of Edmonton, in March 1879. To the kindly fathers there, he unfolded a harrowing tale of despair and starvation. He had taken his wife, mother, brother, and six children into the north woods around the Sturgeon River country, some thirteen kilometres from the mission, for the winter hunt the previous fall. Never had the hunting been so bad, Swift Runner confided. In two months he found nothing to trap or shoot, and by then their initial supply of food was exhausted. Growing weaker with hunger, his family had taken to their beds and attempted to lure friendly squirrels into their grasp. When the supply of squirrels and other small animals had been used up, as a last resort they cut their tent into strips, boiled them and chewed the pieces of rawhide for nourishment. The youngest child was the first to die. With their remaining strength they managed to dig a small grave in the forest. Swift Runner's mother and brother went off by themselves to find food and never returned. His wife, saddened as the other children died one by one, shot herself. Of the party of ten, only Swift Runner survived.

The mission fathers were puzzled by some aspects of

Swift Runner's story. For instance, other Natives returning from the woods brought news of good hunting. Nor did Swift Runner, who weighed nearly ninety-one kilograms, have the appearance of a man who had survived such a terrible ordeal. Nevertheless, they appreciated that hunting could be good in one area but abominable in another, and the torture in the eyes of Swift Runner as he told his lamentable story was very real.

Swift Runner was given food and shelter and invited to stay at the mission. Daily prayers were offered for the tortured soul of the bereaved father, and the little mission settled into its normal routine. As time passed, Swift Runner became a great favourite with the Native children attending school at the mission. He delighted them with tales of hunting in the north woods, or of bygone days when his people, the Crees, had warred with the ferocious Blackfoot Nation to the south. But at night, Swift Runner's dreams were disturbed by the visitations of Ween-de-go. There were times when the priests, watching their strange guest playing with the children, were uneasy.

On the afternoon of May 25, 1879, the Native boys came to Father Kemus, who was in charge of the mission during Father Leduc's absence, seeking permission to accompany Swift Runner on a hunting expedition to the north. Faced with having to make a decision, Father Kemus could no longer suppress his doubts. It was true that Swift Runner had proved himself a gentle man, patient with children, reverent

Swift Runner, or Kak-say-kwyo-chin, in leg
irons with the North West Mounted Police
jailer at Fort Saskatchewan, Alberta, 1879.
GLENBOW ARCHIVES NA-504-1

in his devotions, and obedient to the wishes of the priests, but
the gnawing suspicion was not easily stilled. Withholding
permission, Father Kemus went to the NWMP barracks at
Fort Saskatchewan and laid his problem before the skilled
and experienced scrutiny of Sub-Inspector Severe Gagnon.

Gagnon had already received a circumspect message

from the Native people around Egg Lake, Swift Runner's camping grounds, that the kindly man was one to be watched. Consequently, on hearing Father Kemus's fears, he immediately dispatched Sergeant Richard Steele and interpreter Brazeau to interview Swift Runner. But as they were unable to obtain a coherent report from Swift Runner, Sergeant Steele arrested him and brought him to Fort Saskatchewan on May 27.

Swift Runner's story was that his mother and brother had left, the children had died, one by one, and in the end his wife had killed herself. Sub-Inspector Gagnon was inclined to agree with his sergeant's suspicions, and on June 4, forcing the reluctant Swift Runner to accompany them, he left for the north toward Swift Runner's camp with a party of police.

As they progressed toward the Sturgeon River country, the big Cree's good nature disappeared and he became sullen and stubborn. Twice he tried to escape from evening camps and twice he was recaptured. In earlier interviews, he had volunteered general information about the location of his winter camp, but he now refused to answer all questions. It became evident that he was simply guiding them in a huge circle, and as he was the only one who knew the location of the camp, Gagnon began to despair of ever finding it. It was Brazeau, the interpreter, who solved the problem.

"We'll never get anywhere with that big Indian," Brazeau assured them. "He's too scared and too cunning. We'll give him 'the strong medicine.'"

"No liquor," Gagnon warned.

The interpreter only chuckled and went to prepare a batch of "strong medicine." He started by boiling a brew of tea and then, before the astonished eyes of the policemen, calmly added a large plug of chewing tobacco. He allowed the concoction to brew overnight.

The following morning Brazeau presented the evil-smelling concoction to Swift Runner. He drank it with great gusto. Within a short while his good spirits resumed, then he began to talk and led the police to a clearing on a small, heavily wooded island in the middle of a lake. "This is where we camped," he informed them. "But as you can see, the bears have come and devoured the bodies."

With Swift Runner under close guard, Gagnon and his men began a thorough investigation of the camp. Strewn about the clearing and in the fringes of the trees they found the skulls of eight human beings. Around the campground were human bones, pieces of skin and knots of human hair. Suddenly, Sergeant Steele was horrified by the discovery of a pair of baby's stockings stuffed into the eye socket of one of the skulls. They knew instantly that this was no depredation by prowling bears, but that they stood in the presence of a multiple murderer. As if to confirm their suspicions, they failed to find either bear tracks or claw marks. The teepee, supposed to have been eaten by the starving Indians, was located in the branches of a spruce tree some distance from the campsite. A few kilometres away, hidden in a clump of willow by the lakeshore, they found a kettle, its insides thick with fat. Certain now of the horrible truth, Sub-Inspector Gagnon ordered all the evidence carefully preserved and returned to Fort Saskatchewan to arraign Swift Runner for murder.

On August 16, 1879, Swift Runner was tried before Stipendiary Magistrate Richardson, assisted by two Justices of the Peace—E. McGillivray and George Verey. The jury of six comprised four men fluent in both English and Cree. On the witness stand, Swift Runner changed his story, admitting that he had killed five of his six children as well as his wife. The sixth child had died of starvation. He stuck to his story that his mother and brother had left the party earlier.

After a trial that lasted two days, Swift Runner was found guilty. It took the jury only twenty minutes to decide that he had indeed killed his mother as well as his brother. Judge Richardson then sentenced him to be hanged on December 20, 1879.

In the guardroom while awaiting execution, Swift Runner was still troubled by the nightly visits of Ween-de-go. Father Kemus, who visited him almost daily, could do little to ease his soul. Toward the end of December, Father Leduc returned to Fort Saskatchewan and personally took over the ministrations to Swift Runner. Wise in the ways of his superstitious charges, Father Leduc warned him that he would never be free of his frightful nightmares until he told the truth about the hunting expedition.

Convinced, Swift Runner told a tale whose horror will

seldom be matched in the annals of crime. Father Leduc translated it as follows:

We were camped in the woods about eight miles from here. In the beginning of winter we had not much to suffer. Game was plenty. I killed many moose and five or six bears; but about the middle of February I fell sick and to complete our misfortune those with me could find nothing to shoot. We had soon to kill our dogs and lived on their flesh while it lasted. Having recovered a little from my weakness, I travelled to a post in the Hudson's Bay Company on the Athabasca River and was assisted by the officer in charge, and returned to my camp with a small amount of provisions. That did not last us long. We all—that is, my mother, wife and six children (three boys and three girls) besides my brother and I—began to feel the pangs of hunger. My brother made up his mind to start with my mother in search of some game. I remained alone with my family. Starvation became worse and worse. For many days we had nothing to eat. I advised my wife to start with the children and follow on the snow and tracks of my mother and brother, who perhaps had been lucky enough to kill a moose or a bear since they left us. For my part, though weak, I hoped that remaining alone I could support my life with my gun. All my family left me with the exception of a little boy, ten years of age.

I remained many days with my boy without finding any game and consequently without having a mouthful to eat. One morning I got up early and suddenly an abominable thought crossed my mind. My son was lying down close to the fire, fast asleep. Pushed by the evil spirits, I took my poor gun and shot him. The ball entered the top of his skull. Still he breathed. I began to cry, but what was the use. I then took my knife and sunk it twice into his side. Alas, he still breathed and I picked up a stick and killed him with it. I then satisfied my hunger by eating some of his flesh and lived on that for some days, extracting even the marrow from the bones.

For some days afterwards, I wandered through the woods. Unfortunately, I met my wife and children. I said to them that my son had died of starvation but I noticed immediately that they suspected the frightening reality.

They then told me that they had not seen either my mother or brother. No doubt both had died of starvation, otherwise they would have been heard of, as it is now seven months since then. Three days after joining my family, the oldest of my boys died. We dug a grave with an axe and buried him. We were then reduced to boiling some pieces of our leather tent, our shoes and buffalo robes, in order to keep ourselves alive.

I discovered that my family wanted to leave me from fear of meeting the same fate as my boy. One morning I got up early, and I don't know why—I was mad. It seems to me that all the devils had entered my heart. My wife and children were asleep around me. Pushed by the evil spirit, I took my gun, and placing the muzzle against her, shot her. I then without delay took my hatchet and massacred my three little girls. There was now but one little boy, seven years old, surviving. I awoke him and told him to melt some snow for water at once. The poor child was so weakened by long fasting to make any reflection of the frightful spectacle under his eyes. I took the bodies of my little girls and cut them up. I did the same with the corpse of my wife. I broke the skulls and took out the brains, and broke up the bones in order to get the marrow. My little son and I lived for seven or eight days on the flesh—I eating the flesh of my wife and children, he the flesh of his mother and sisters.

At length I left there all the bones and started with the last of my family. Snow began to melt now. Spring had commenced. Ducks arrived and flew every day around us, and I could find enough to live upon, but I felt reluctant to see people. I then told my son that after some days we would meet people; they will know very soon that I am a murderer, and they will certainly make me die. As to you there is no fear; say all you know; no harm will be done to you. One day I had killed many ducks. I was a few miles from Egg Lake, where some relations of mine lived. I was sitting at the camp fire, when I told my son to go and fetch something five or six paces off. At that moment the devil suddenly took possession of my soul; and in order to live longer far from people, and to put out of the way the only witness to my crimes, I seized my gun and killed the last of my children and ate him as I did the others. Some weeks after I was taken by the police, sentenced to death, and in three days I am to be hanged.

Swift Runner's story, as told to Father Leduc, cleared up one mystery for the police. Ten people had gone into the woods that winter and only one had come out alive. However, only eight skulls had been found at the "starvation camp," leaving one person unaccounted for. The gruesome account of the last child's death was the missing link, for, despite what he confessed to Father Leduc, Swift Runner had already admitted to the police that he had killed and eaten his brother and his mother, who, he said ruefully, had been a bit tough.

With his confession, Swift Runner became a changed man. Ween-de-go no longer tormented him. He felt ready to embrace the faith of the Fathers who had befriended him at St. Albert Mission and made whatever peace he could with man and the white man's God.

The execution of Swift Runner presented special problems. To the Natives and many of the Metis in the district, hanging was particularly disagreeable. They believed it "a death fit only for a dog." They believed, too, that hanging consisted of lifting a body up, holding it there and cutting it to pieces. Even Swift Runner, a big man, is said to have made merry at the thought of the hangman lifting him up to the rope.

Sheriff Richards, who lived at Battleford, made the long journey overland in the dead of winter for the execution. He reached Fort Saskatchewan on the evening of December 19, just in time to read the death warrant to the condemned man. Swift Runner received this news with a smile.

The morning of the execution dawned clear, with the temperature at forty-two degrees below zero. Sergeant Fred Bagley, who had come west with the North West Mounted Police (NWMP) on its original march, was in charge of execution detail. At first no one would act as executioner and it appeared that Sheriff Richards would have to perform the melancholy function himself. But at the last moment, an old army pensioner named Rogers agreed to act.

Though Swift Runner had ignored the banging of the fort's carpenter as the scaffold was being constructed outside the guardroom, he examined it with great interest as he was led from his cell just after 10 A.M. When placed on the trap, Swift Runner paid little heed as Rogers strapped his arms and legs. Instead he launched into a speech thanking the police for their kindness and the Fathers for their mercy. To the fifty or so spectators gathered for the West's first execution, he reiterated that he knew he had done wrong. As he finished speaking, he shivered in the cold and, turning to the executioner, began to scold him for keeping him waiting so long in the chill air.

The groan of the trap door and the "swack" of the hangman's noose cut short his scolding. Swift Runner plunged through the opening and died instantly—the first person legally executed under the jurisdiction of the NWMP. "It was," summarized Jim Reade, one of the onlookers and a veteran of the California gold rush of 1849, "the purtiest hangin' I ever seen and it's the twenty-ninth."

4

Manitoba's First Outlaw

THE DISTINCTION OF BEING MANITOBA'S first official outlaw goes to Gilbert Godon, a stout, poker-faced young Metis from Red Lake district. He came into prominence in the troubled times that followed the first Riel uprising of 1869–70. There was a great deal of ill feeling between the occupation troops sent from Canada and the Metis of Fort Garry and St. Boniface. Godon, a man of quick movement and decisive action, allied himself with the soldiers and was frequently found swinging his fists or a bottle on their behalf.

A favourite off-duty haunt for the soldiers was the Pride of the West Saloon in Fort Garry (now Winnipeg), operated by Dugald Sinclair. It was also frequented by

Metis. Usually the two groups managed to avoid each other—the soldiers by visiting during the day and the Metis in the evening—but occasionally their visits coincided and invariably led to friction.

During a pitched battle between Metis and soldiers on one of these occasions, someone pulled a revolver and fired at innkeeper Sinclair, who was vainly trying to halt the melee. Gilbert Godon flung himself on the would-be assassin and took the bullet intended for Sinclair in his right arm. A few minutes later, reinforcements arrived from the barracks and the Metis left. Godon's wound was treated by a local doctor and the whole incident was written off by the police of the recently formed province of Manitoba as a demonstration of youthful exuberance.

Drinking and brawling continued to be popular pastimes at Red River during the early 1870s, and Godon was frequently found in the middle of these activities. Nothing unduly serious happened until the night of October 10, 1873, when Godon and a group of drinking pals arrived at the Dufferin home of A.J. Fawcett, who sold liquor illegally. Most of the group had already tilted the bottle high at a similar outlet, and when Fawcett refused to serve them he was pushed and threatened by Benjamin Marchand, who promised violence if the whisky was not produced quickly.

Godon, with his penchant for defending bartenders, intervened and chased Marchand outside. Marchand's son, Benjamin, retaliated by seizing a shovel and banging it lustily

Upper Fort Garry, 1870s.
WILLIAM JAMES TOPLEY, LIBRARY AND ARCHIVES CANADA, PA-009839

on Godon's head. A wild slugfest erupted, rattling the bottles in the cellar. The Godon faction, which included his brother and his father, gained the decisive edge and the Marchands retreated to the backyard. They regrouped and made a second assault but were repelled.

With Godon and his allies victorious, Fawcett suddenly remembered that he did have some whisky in the cellar. The chairs were righted, and the guests settled down. About an hour later, however, Godon went outside to clear his head and found young Benjamin in the backyard. Thinking the youth was organizing another attack on the house, he dragged him inside. Godon, who towered over Marchand, knocked him down several times and then, with his opponent lying helpless on the floor, seized an axe and struck him on the head with the back of the blade.

One man tried to intervene, but before he could come between Godon and his victim, Godon struck Marchand a fatal blow with the blade. Since there was neither doctor nor police closer than Fort Garry, ninety-five kilometres to the north, Fawcett went to the nearby headquarters of the Canadian Boundary Commission. He returned with a party of fifteen men led by Sergeant James H. Armstrong of the Royal Engineers. Benjamin Marchand died shortly after their arrival.

Godon surrendered quietly and was held overnight. But when the officer in charge of the Boundary Commission refused to accept responsibility for detaining him, he was released and immediately fled across the border into Dakota Territory.

Meanwhile, a coroner's jury returned a verdict that Marchand had died at the hand of Gilbert Godon. On November 12, 1873, a grand jury brought in a true bill of murder against him. When he did not appear to answer the charge, a bench warrant was issued for his arrest. But issuing a warrant was far easier than serving it. In the early days of the West, there was little co-operation between law enforcement authorities in Manitoba and Dakota Territory. There simply weren't enough policemen on either side of the line to permit the luxury of outlaw hunting. Wanted men fled either north or south of the border and were safe as long as they remained peaceable.

Unfortunately for Godon, remaining peaceful proved

impossible. He was involved in a fight six months after arriving in Dakota Territory and thrown in Pembina jail, just south of the border. When Chief Constable Richard Power of the MPP learned of this development, he left for the US. The American lawmen were quite willing to relinquish their prisoner, and after several days of hard travelling Power returned to Winnipeg with the murder suspect. The same day, June 19, 1874, Godon was arraigned and pleaded not guilty.

Frontier justice moved swiftly. The following Monday he was tried for murder. After a jury deliberation of only thirty minutes, he was found guilty and sentenced to hang on August 26. A reporter at the trial described Godon as being "about 22 years of age, 6'2" in height and stout in proportion. Taken on the whole his face is rather unprepossessing. His forehead is what might be called massive, his eyes sunk deeply into his head and his whole features are devoid of expression. Throughout the whole trial he paid little attention and when the death sentence was passed he simply yawned, stretched himself as though tired of sitting in the dock and announced himself ready to go back to his cell." Godon shared the death cell with Joseph Michaud, a twenty-three-year-old gunner of the Dominion Artillery. Michaud was due to hang on August 24 for the stabbing death of a passerby who had tried to intervene in a fight between a drink-crazed Michaud and another soldier.

Godon had the sympathy of at least one man. Pride

of the West owner Dugald Sinclair, whose life Godon had saved in 1870, began a campaign to obtain clemency for his young friend. In response to petitions, the Canadian government commuted Godon's sentence to fourteen years' imprisonment. Cellmate Michaud was not so fortunate. He was hanged in public at Winnipeg in August 1874, with so many citizens wanting to see the event that many were unable to obtain tickets.

After Godon's sentence was commuted he was transferred to the provincial penitentiary at Upper Fort Garry. Although he seemed resigned to serving his long sentence, he was merely biding his time. On the morning of September 25, 1876, he suddenly broke from his place at the woodpile where he was working and ran toward a small boat moored on the nearby Red River. Despite a rapid volley from surprised prison guards, he escaped unscathed into the woods on the east bank.

News travelled slowly in the sparsely settled community, there being neither telephone nor telegraph, and Godon had no difficulty in collecting his horse and his wife. He again fled into Dakota Territory. By October 10, the official search for him had been given up.

For nearly a year, the young outlaw flitted between Pembina and his brother's home at Emerson, just north of the boundary. He faced few risks doing so. On the Canadian side there were only a few provincial policemen, while on the American side no lawman was going to look for a

Canadian desperado unless there was a suitable reward. But on August 18, 1877, word reached F.T. Bradley, Justice of the Peace at Emerson, that Godon was planning to visit his brother. Bradley deputized brothers William and John Lucas and sent them with his bailiff, Williams, to attempt an arrest.

At Emerson, William Lucas, in command of the miniature posse, posted the bailiff to guard a side entrance to David Godon's log house and his brother to watch the front door. Then William burst into the house and found himself confronted by the wanted man, a loaded revolver in each hand. Before William could react, Godon's mother and sister-in-law launched themselves on him, and while he warded off the blows and kicks of the screaming women, Godon slipped quickly through the side door, surprising and disarming the bailiff. He tossed the posseman's rifle into a clump of bushes and walked nonchalantly toward dense underbrush flanking the river.

Months passed with no word of the fugitive. Then in late February 1880, Godon's passion for drinking and brawling again betrayed him. During a drinking party at Pembina, he became involved in a dispute with Alexander Montreault and broke five of his ribs. Godon was arrested by the Dakota police on a charge of assault with intent to kill and lodged in Pembina's log prison.

Godon shared the crude frontier lock-up with two men—Frank Larose, charged with poisoning his wife, and

T.P. Murray, a lightning-rod salesman held on charges of fraud and embezzlement. The three spent their days cutting wood with a bucksaw for the lock-up's pot-bellied stoves and their evenings planning an escape. As part of the plan, they smuggled a used bucksaw blade into their cells.

The opportunity came on the night of June 25, 1880. The night watchman fell ill and had to go home. Before a replacement could be sent to the prison, the three men had unearthed the bucksaw blade, sawn a section in the ceiling, and pulled themselves into the office above. From there it was a simple matter to force the front door and walk into the night. At 3 A.M. the small settlement was deserted, and the men made their way undetected to a Native camp on the Red River. Finding several unattended canoes, they stole two and paddled away.

Murray, seeking Canadian sanctuary, paddled to Winnipeg. Here he loudly protested his innocence of the charges against him in the United States. He also forsook his job as lightning-rod salesman and became a successful and respected real-estate dealer in the community.

Meanwhile, Godon, now wanted on both sides of the border, fled westward with Frank Larose. Some five months later a fragmentary report indicated that Godon and Larose had reached the sanctuary of a Metis camp on the Missouri River but Larose had died shortly after their arrival, of exposure and hunger. Of Gilbert Godon, the Canadian West's first Indigenous outlaw, nothing more is known.

5

Calgary's First Hanging

MALCOLM MCNEIL STOPPED THE BAY team in front of McKelvie's store in the newly established foothills community of Calgary and threw the reins to his companions. Promising not to keep them waiting long in the crisp February night, he slid from the sleigh seat, rubbed some circulation back into his chilled limbs, and walked across the sidewalk covered with new-fallen snow. It was 8:30 P.M. on Friday, February 8, 1884.

A little bell tinkled gently as he opened the door of the grocery store, but there was no sign of life. McNeil unbuttoned his heavy sheepskin coat as he walked to the counter. "Mr. McKelvie?" There was no answer.

McNeil looked around the store. "Jim Adams?" Then he

saw the crumpled figure behind the counter. "Jim! Sleeping on the job? What will old man McKelvie . . . " McNeil stopped short, gripped by terror. The head of the man he thought was asleep lay in a pool of blood.

McNeil spun back to the door. "Spearon! Hogg! Come in here. Jim's hurt himself!"

His two hunting companions joined him to stare in disbelief at the scene. Then, with the natural distrust of death and violence that most men possess, the trio backed slowly to the doorway. As they did, a man named Fraser who operated a confectionery store adjacent to the grocery pushed through the door. "What's going on here," he demanded. "Somebody said Jim Adams was hurt."

"See for yourself," McNeil pointed to the body of the young man. "Jim's done himself in."

Fraser looked at the body. One glance was enough to see the gaping wound in the man's neck. "Incredible," he muttered. "He was in my store just half an hour ago to borrow a pitcher of water for his tea. Chipper as a squirrel. Well, we'd better get the police."

When the report of the suicide came into the NWMP at Calgary, Inspector Sam Steele detailed Inspector Tom Dowling and Dr. Kennedy to investigate. Arriving at the McKelvie store they discovered that a group of citizens had already gathered and that the affair had taken a different turn. What at first looked like a simple case of suicide was obviously cold-blooded murder.

While Dr. Kennedy knelt to examine the still warm body, Inspector Dowling questioned those present. From store owner McKelvie, hastily summoned from a church meeting, he learned that the victim was a young Scot from New Brunswick who filled in as a part-time clerk. McNeil, still shaken from the shock of his discovery, told of finding the body and said he had not noticed anyone near the store when they drove up in the sleigh.

Inspecting the premises, Dowling saw that the cash drawer was partly open and empty. A question to McKelvie revealed that it should have contained nearly $50. Another clue was found at the rear exit, where a small chopping axe, its head and handle covered with blood, lay partly concealed behind a packing box. Nearby, a dollar bill was caught under the door.

Dr. Kennedy finished examining the body. "As close as I can determine," he told Inspector Dowling, "Adams had his back to the assailant. His attacker leaped upon him, probably threw an arm around his head, and slashed his throat with a sharp instrument. There are no signs of a struggle on his body. Whatever the instrument was, it made a slight cut on the left side of the neck, then dug deeply on the right side, severing the windpipe, the major arteries, and leaving a gash about six inches in length. From the position of two cuts on the back of his head, I would suggest that he was struck after he fell to the floor."

"No sign of a struggle," Dowling commented. "Attacked

from behind, probably as he opened the cash register. Looks as if he knew his attacker."

"He certainly had no warning," Dr. Kennedy agreed.

Inspector Dowling sent to the police barracks for more men, and then began a closer examination of the crowd for possible witnesses. One, Ed Francis, said that he had been in the store earlier that evening to chat with Adams. While there, he remembered that Jess Williams, a black man who worked as a cook at the Far West Hotel, had come in to pay a bill. It resulted in a small fuss. Williams had gone behind the counter and personally scratched his name off the list of those who owed money. Adams told him that he should not have come behind the counter, and Williams had gone out muttering that when he paid a debt he wanted proof it was paid. He had quite obviously been drinking. Neither Francis nor Adams was upset by the incident.

Fraser, the confectionery store owner, then recalled that while they were waiting for the police to arrive, Williams had come to the store to ask what the excitement was. On being told that Adams was dead, he had simply made a commonplace remark and left, showing no further interest in the affair. Although there was as yet nothing to connect Williams with the brutal murder, he was already a prime suspect. Francis, wittingly or unwittingly, had aroused suspicions when he remarked that when Williams went behind the store counter, he had had ample opportunity to see how much money was in the till.

Calgary's Stephen Avenue, 1884. Fraser's Confectionery store is to the right; McKelvie's store is to the left. GLENBOW NA-1931-1

With the arrival of reinforcements from the detachment, Inspector Dowling took prompt action. He cleared the store and re-examined it, but found nothing to add to the meagre bits of information gathered thus far. His conclusion was that an assailant, or assailants, had tricked Adams into opening the cash drawer, attacked him with a sharp instrument, and beaten him with the axe before fleeing through the back door—if the evidence of the dollar bill was to be credited.

Since a wave of antagonism was already being stirred up against Williams, and men were beginning to mutter about lynch laws, Dowling dispatched Sergeant-Major Blake with a posse of police to find the suspect.

Feelings were now running high in the little frontier community. In his biography, *Forty Years in Canada,* Inspector Sam Steele wrote of the incident:

The murder caused a great deal of excitement, and when it was reported a large mob of citizens, headed by a very decent but excited individual, came to find out what I was going to do about it, and there were threats of lynching the perpetrator if captured. But I said to him, "You lads are all tenderfeet, and have visions before you of taking part in a Neck-tie Social. There never has been a lynching in Canada, nor will there be as long as our force has the police duties to perform, so go away like sensible men, and remember that any attempt at lynching will be bad for those who try it!" This settled the matter.

Blake's posse had no difficulty locating the shack where Jess Williams lived with his common-law wife, Religious, a Sarcee woman, and his Native brother-in-law and wife. After posting his men, Blake knocked on the door. It was opened by the suspect himself.

"Jess, I want to talk to you about the killing of young Adams."

"Don't know nothing about it, except what I heard down at the store," Williams informed him blandly.

"We want to search your house," Blake informed him, pushing inside.

"I had nothing to do with that," Williams said.

Inside the shack, while Religious and the other Natives watched in apprehensive silence, Blake examined the man's clothing. On a coat he found a splash of still wet blood.

"How did you get this, Jess?" the policeman demanded.

"Oh, that must be from the beef I carried back from the butcher's place," Williams protested. "You can find the meat in a box at the back of the shack."

Blake found the parcel of meat, neatly wrapped, but there was no indication that it had leaked blood. "Jess Williams," he said, "I am arresting you on suspicion of the murder of James Adams. I'll have to take you down to the barracks."

Leaving the two men to question the Natives, Blake escorted his prisoner to Calgary barracks. Here, additional bloodstains were found on Williams's clothing, and imprinted against the cloth of a pants pocket was the outline of what one officer suggested might be a case of some kind. While this examination was taking place, a constable returned from the shack with a damning piece of evidence. Shortly after the murder, Williams had arrived at the shack and ordered his wife to heat water to wash some blood from his hands.

A strong guard was placed over the suspect that night, and with the breaking of the cold February dawn, police checked for further evidence. Constable McRae discovered a set of footprints leading away from the back door of the store. Following them, he quickly located a blood-stained razor and, farther on, a blood-smeared razor case. Recalling that the imprint of such a case had been found on the inside of Jess Williams's pocket, the constable carefully wrapped his grim evidence.

The trail led down the back alley, past the offices of the *Calgary Herald*, and toward the Elbow River to the south. Near the butcher's shed on the Cochrane Ranch, McRae found a bloodstained leather glove. From here, the tracks led to a road that had been traversed several times since the previous night, thus obliterating the footprints. Later, however, the glove was identified by Williams's wife as being the same kind worn by him. In addition, the print from his overshoes matched perfectly those found in the snow behind McKelvie's store.

Even though confronted with this additional circumstantial evidence, Jess Williams loudly continued to voice his innocence. He talked quite freely of himself and told how he had been born in Texas in 1841 and moved north to Detroit after the Civil War. From there he drifted to Canada, where he worked as a cook for construction crews on the CPR, a job that eventually brought him west. After the completion of the railway, he worked as a cook on a ranch, and in late 1883 came to Calgary. Again, he was employed as a cook for two months, but for the past two weeks had been out of work.

On the night of the murder, Williams admitted he had been drinking but declined to name the man who sold him the liquor. He admitted going to the store and having a mild argument with Adams, but denied killing him. After his visit to McKelvie's store he went to the butcher's shop, paid a small bill, bought some beef—from which he obtained the telltale bloodstains—and heard a commotion at McKelvie's store. On going there, he learned that Adams had committed suicide or been murdered. It being no business of his, he said, he had returned home.

At this point, the first break came. Williams admitted that the glove found near the butcher's shop was his. Unknown to him, some ranch hands on the nearby Cochrane Ranch had discovered the mate to the glove stuffed under some hay on a hayrack. Inside the glove was the stolen money—less than $50, for which Adams had wantonly been slain. Evidently, when fleeing the store the killer had thrust the money into the glove and concealed it in the hay, intending to return for it later. Pure chance had revealed its hiding place.

With great reluctance, Williams admitted that this was the mate to the glove found beside the footprints in the snow, but feebly tried to protest than an unknown stranger had given him the money and told him to hide it. Following this explanation, he requested an interview with Inspector Dowling.

He confessed that he had killed Adams, then afterward gave an interview with Thomas B. Brayden, who the year before had co-founded a newspaper with the impressive name *The Calgary Herald, Mining and Ranche Advocate and General Advertiser*. On February 14, 1884, the paper published Williams's interview:

I have confessed the crime to the Commanding Officer voluntarily, and I may as well tell you. On Friday night I went to McKelvie's store to settle a little bill I owed, and saw deceased and another gentleman present; after paying the account I asked deceased for a pencil which was given me. I went forward and scratched out the account which was recorded on the wall; deceased said I should not have done this; I answered the debt was paid, and I wanted it blotted out.

The other gentleman then went out; deceased and I began wrestling or fooling, and in the fray, Mr. Adams received a slight hurt, and got angry, saying that this must be stopped or there would be a fuss. I said there was no fear of a fuss; seeing a razor on the counter I picked it up and struck at him, not meaning to hurt him, but cut a gash on the left side of his throat.

Seeing I had injured him more than I intended, I thought I would finish him, which I did with the razor; I then went out but seeing no one, I came back, and as the deceased seemed to be suffering, I picked up the axe and struck him with it to put him out of pain; I then went to the drawer and took out the money; went to the bank of the Elbow River and hid it; I then started for home.

Feelings were running high in the little frontier town of Calgary, and the police quickly brought Williams before a court. On February 20, the trial was held before Judge Macleod, former commissioner of the NWMP, and a jury comprised of some of Calgary's leading citizens. Throughout the trial Williams listened impassively to the evidence. At times he smiled, though the effect was marred by a cast in his left eye that gave his face a sinister appearance.

He was well defended by a lawyer named James A. Lougheed, but the evidence was overwhelming and the jury found him guilty without leaving the box. Judge Macleod sentenced Williams to hang on March 29, less than two months after he had committed the crime.

"Some weeks later the sentence of the court was carried out," Sam Steele wrote, "the prisoner marching to the scaffold with a jaunty, military step, keeping time with the escort, and on the scaffold he faced the witnesses to the execution, and stated that drink was the cause of the crime. Dr. Kennedy and I were the official witnesses, and I relate these circumstances for the reason that this was the first execution in the North West Territories of any person other than an Indian, and it was carried out in the barrack square of the Mounted Police."

6

Prairie Stagecoach Holdups

Alberta's First Stagecoach Robbery

The Calgary–Edmonton Trail was an historic ribbon of road. The missionary McDougalls—father and son—drove the first herd of domestic cattle over it in 1874 from Fort Edmonton to Morley. Throughout the early 1870s illegal whisky traders from Forts Whoop-Up, Slide Out, and Stand Off traversed it with their wagonloads of firewater and furs, and the Alberta Field Force moved up it in 1885 on their way to overtake Big Bear and the murderers of Frog Lake settlers during the Riel Rebellion. Many strange and fascinating conveyances passed over the old trail, including Native travois, dog teams, and Red River carts. Then, between 1883 and 1891, it was travelled by the stagecoaches that connected the fledgling communities of Edmonton and Calgary.

The first stagecoach left Edmonton on August 6, 1883— one month before the CPR reached Calgary. An enterprising old-timer from Edmonton, Donald MacLeod, started the passenger and mail service between the two prairie settlements. Known as one of the old Northwest's hospitable characters, MacLeod had been a Red River settler before travelling the Carlton Trail in 1875 and settling down as a part-time trader-prospector in Edmonton. His house was always open to friend or visitor. Many a discouraged prospector sponged a meal from Donald MacLeod. The only payment demanded was an interesting story or two. He was a man of strong physique and character and respected by all who had contact with him. He was also a shrewd businessman with a firm belief in the destiny of the West.

His stage usually left Edmonton on a Monday morning from the hitching rail in front of Jasper House. The trip took five days—perhaps—with night rests at such stopping places as Peach Hills, Battle River, Red Deer Crossing, and Willow Creek. There were also numerous watering places with picturesque names like Scarletts, Blindman, and Bear's Hill. In theory, the stage was to arrive in Calgary on a Friday night, but travel was rather unpredictable and it might be hours or even days late. After a weekend layover in Calgary, the stage started back from the HBC store at 9 A.M. on Monday. A round trip normally took two weeks, although veteran stage travellers knew that this schedule was extremely flexible. For this reason, patience was a valuable asset for passengers on the Edmonton–Calgary route and others in western Canada.

In 1883 Archdeacon J.W. Tims came to Alberta from England. He eventually reached Fort Benton in Montana Territory and noted, "At Fort Benton I had to stay six days until the I.G. Baker Express [an open wagon drawn by four mules] was ready to make its bi-monthly trip to [Fort] Macleod." From Fort Benton to Fort Macleod was just over 320 kilometres, the trip taking eight days. "There were no bridges crossing the rivers," the archdeacon noted, "no fences of any kind and no roads, the only trails being those made by the ox-teams."

At Fort Macleod, the archdeacon discovered another aspect of Western travel—accommodation was bare-boned. The party stayed at a restaurant run by a black woman called Aunty. He wrote,

> It was a long building, one storey in height, with a lean-to at the far end which served as kitchen and Aunty's bedroom. The sleepers provided their own blankets, and slept on the floor. About six a.m. Aunty appeared with a broom, poked each sleeper with it, and told them to get up and roll up their bedding. Then, from the far end of the room, she commenced to sweep the floor and expected everyone to be up with blankets rolled by the time she reached them.

Prairie Stagecoach Holdups

The stagecoach drivers were a special breed—tough, resourceful men who have justifiably become part of the Western legend. In its November 23, 1886, edition, the *Macleod Gazette* carried the following tribute to them:

There is no occupation in the world that looks more easy and pleasant at times, and there is none which at other times is more difficult or that requires more care, genuine courage and good management. In the summer, the weather is warm and the rivers easily crossed. When the first cold weather comes, the hills are slippery and the rivers mean, and then it is that the stage driver requires all the self possession, nerve and skill that nature may have endowed him with . . .

At the head of the list of Northwest drivers, Frank Pollinger reigns supreme. Frank is known and admired from Winnipeg to the Rocky Mountains, and north as far as Frenchman's Butte, where he took part in that memorable battle. He has driven over nearly all the four- and six-horse stage routes in the Western states, where his reputation is just as high as it is here. Every horse in his team knows him, and a word from him is as good as a club in the average driver's hands. Frank is a deserved favourite, and the average passenger considers himself in good luck if he gets a seat alongside of him—except in cold and stormy weather, when Polly generally has to hold it down alone unless there is a full house.

All the others are good drivers and good fellows. The stage driver has generally a very keen sense of his duty. He will always do more for his employers and his horses than he will for himself. The last trip in from Benton, the driver got into difficulty in the river at Frank Strong's Crossing. With the thermometer down below zero, he worked in water nearly up to his waist for some two hours. Without getting dry or warm, he came straight through to Macleod, arriving after dark in the evening, and encased in a solid mass of ice. Even then he delivered his mail and would not stir from his seat until he had made every endeavor to report to the collector of customs. It was a long time before he could thaw out his clothes sufficiently to get them off.

J.D. Higginbotham was a frequent stagecoach passenger during Alberta's frontier era. He established the first drugstore in Lethbridge and wrote a most interesting book, *When the West Was Young*. He wrote of one stagecoach trip with Polly Pollinger:

Needless to say at this period, the streams were devoid of bridges, although ferries crossed High River, also the Old Man near Macleod; but all others we were obliged to ford and sometimes swim. The passengers and mail were put on the "hurricane deck" of the coach, which, having a high and sloping dashboard, was fairly well adapted for amphibious purposes; however, we usually landed on the opposite bank some distance down-stream from where we entered the water. The drivers were artists in their line and seemed to know these quickly-changing fords by instinct. One of them, the famous "Polly," made the boast to me that he could drive his coach and four where I "couldn't trail a whip." Years later he had sufficient confidence in me to allow me to handle the "ribbons" for him on a good piece of trail, while he peacefully slept off a race-day spree on top of the mail sacks . . .

These men were heavy drinkers, and in those so-called "prohibition days" took their "red-eye" straight. In winter, when the trail was obscured by snow, it might easily be rediscovered by the presence of "dead soldiers" along the route. These were headless—or neckless—bottles, as the drivers scorned the use of corkscrews, or openers, and simply decapitated them upon the sharp steel tires of the coach.

Despite the drivers' fondness for "red-eye" they were able to cope with hazards which included blizzards, sub-zero temperatures, prairie fires, floods, and irate passengers. But on August 23, 1886, a new hazard appeared.

The Calgary–Edmonton stage, with driver Braden in charge, left the HBC store that morning on time, forded the Bow River, and headed for Fort Edmonton. About twenty-four kilometres north of Calgary, two armed horsemen forced Braden to stop. Both men were masked— one with a piece of the Union Jack flag and the other with a black cloth. Meeting with no resistance, the holdup men first cut open the mail sacks. When they found nothing of importance they relieved the startled driver and passenger of their valuables. Braden was then ordered to drive on while the men mounted and rode west toward the Rocky Mountains.

Although the holdup had taken place just after noon and only a short distance from Calgary's police barracks, it

Calgary–Edmonton Stagecoach crossing a mudhole, 1888.
GLENBOW ARCHIVE NA-1162-3

was not until 5:30 P.M. that word reached Inspector Antrobus of the NWMP. Even then the news was relayed by a passenger rather than the stagecoach company's office. The reason was discovered later. Driver Braden, after retrieving the discarded mail sacks, had decided to resume the trip and suggested that since the mails were intact it was up to the passengers to report their own losses.

From the passenger's description of the bandits, the superintendent was struck by the resemblance between them and two men who had robbed the De Rainbouville brothers at Elbow River, southwest of Calgary, a short time before. Assembling a posse of seventeen police and civilian volunteers, Antrobus left for the site of the robbery. He found little in the way of evidence except two sets of hoof prints leading westward through the tall grass. The superintendent led his posse in pursuit.

They had not gone far from the trail before the grass grew shorter and the ground too hard to hold a set of prints. However, as signs indicated that the bandits had stopped at this point, Antrobus ordered a thorough search. One of the posse soon found a pair of dusty overalls and a piece of flag partly concealed beneath a large boulder. Another, who had done prison guard duty at the barracks, recognized the overalls as those worn by John Young, a man recently released after serving six months for possession of illegal liquor.

Antrobus suspected that the holdup men would return to Calgary by one of the back trails. He divided his party into three—one group to ride westward and then circle south, a second to ride eastward and also circle south, and the third led by Antrobus to cover both sides of the Calgary–Edmonton Trail. In this way, a strip some twenty kilometres wide was scoured from the site of the robbery to the outskirts of Calgary. Homesteaders, cowboys, Natives, and townspeople were questioned along the way, but no one had seen the two men. When the three posses reassembled at midnight, their only lead was a report of two strangers at the cabin of Scott Krenger, a prospector at Shaganappi Point, nineteen kilometres west of Calgary.

Krenger, usually called "Clinker Scott," was well known at police headquarters. He never seemed to work, but always managed to survive. When the police called he confirmed that he did indeed have two men staying with him, but they couldn't have robbed the stage since they had been in his cabin all week. Inspector Antrobus dismissed them as immediate suspects, although he kept them in mind.

A search was then undertaken in Calgary for Young, the man whose overalls had been found with the piece of flag. But he had not been seen in his usual haunts since his release from prison.

A few days later, a settler searching for a stolen buckboard visited Krenger's cabin. Although Krenger's horse was tied to the corral, there was no sign of him. The settler peered through the cabin's grimy window and was astonished to see Krenger on the floor, obviously dead. His assailant—or assailants—had surprised him, for his hands were still covered with flour and there was a half-finished pan of biscuit dough on the table. He had been shot in the stomach. The doctor later placed death on August 25, two days after the stagecoach robbery.

The two men seen in Krenger's cabin by the posse on the night of the holdup had disappeared, but when descriptions of them were checked, neither one resembled the elusive Mr. Young. Nevertheless, he remained a prime suspect.

Inspector Antrobus believed that the three crimes were linked, if not all perpetrated by the same two men. The robbery of the De Rainbouville brothers, the stagecoach holdup, and the murder of "Clinker Scott" seemed to form a pattern. It was possible there had been a quarrel over the division of spoils and that the men murdered Krenger as a result. Alternatively, Krenger may have outlived his usefulness to them as a cover.

With this possibility in mind, and realizing that he was dealing with desperate men, Antrobus intensified his efforts by engaging famous railroad detective J.L. Benoit to work on the case. At his suggestion, Sergeant Spicer from the Maple Creek NWMP detachment was made a special investigator.

Disguised as a prospector, Spicer visited mining camps in the hopes of picking up the trail of the fugitives, believed to have holed up in the mountains. Nobody, however, had noticed any suspicious characters. At the same time, Sergeant A.R. MacDonnell circulated through Calgary in plain clothes trying to pick up information that might lead to the wanted men. His task was a risky one, for Calgary was the headquarters of assorted cattle thieves, horse runners, and outlaws. When weeks passed without a clue, it seemed that the "Union Jack" bandits had vanished.

Suspicion did focus briefly on a William Mitchell, who was arrested and tried for the De Rainbouville brothers' robbery but acquitted by a jury. With no further evidence, Detective Benoit felt he could no longer be of use, and Sergeants Spicer and MacDonnell were given other assignments. Antrobus let it be known that the case was closed.

Hoping this ruse would either bring the wanted men

out of hiding or start idle tongues wagging, Antrobus waited a month before assigning an undercover policeman not known to Calgary's criminal element. But while several hints led him to believe the men were hiding in British Columbia, none proved substantial and the undercover man was removed from duty.

On December 15, 1886, the elusive John Young surrendered to the NWMP. He came complete with an airtight alibi and as a result was not charged with any of the offences. Alberta's first—and only—stagecoach holdup was never solved, proving to be the perfect crime.

Saskatchewan's Unlikely Stagecoach Bandit

On the morning of July 12, 1886, George L. Garnett, ferryman for the South Branch crossing of the Saskatchewan River, hitched up his bay mare. He kissed his wife goodbye, gave last-minute instructions to the relief ferryman he had hired and drove off into the pages of history. He was about to undertake Saskatchewan's first and only stagecoach holdup.

Four days later, Garnett showed up at Salt Springs, some sixty-five kilometres south of Humboldt on the Qu'Appelle–Prince Albert Trail. Salt Springs was an important way station for the mail drivers since the southbound stage from Prince Albert met and exchanged passengers and mail with the north-bound coaches from the CPR mainline at Qu'Appelle. At 7 P.M. on July 16, both stages arrived on schedule and laid over for the night. Shortly after their arrival, Garnett rode north out of town.

He was up with the sun and left after a hasty breakfast. From time to time he stopped on a hill to survey the back trail, but there was no sign of the north-bound stage. Then, a few kilometres north of Salt Springs, he came upon five men asleep in their camp beside the trail.

There had been nothing in the career of George L. Garnett to account for what he did next. Born in London, Ontario, he had come west during the 1885 Riel Rebellion. After serving with the 7th Fusiliers, he settled in Winnipeg, where he married and then moved to South Branch to run the ferry. Well respected by his neighbours and a devout churchman, he had added to his esteem by operating the ferry efficiently—a rarity in those days. He was to prove an equally efficient holdup man, beginning with the five sleeping men.

When there was no response to his summons, Garnett fired two shots into the air. Almost at once the sleepy men, still suffering the effects of too much whisky the night before, tumbled into the morning sunlight. They blinked in surprise at the unmasked bandit. Pretending to have a partner concealed nearby, Garnett relieved them of their wallets and loose change, close to $300, then left.

Toward 1 P.M., about forty kilometres south of Humboldt, Garnett stopped the Prince Albert stage. It was driven by John Art and carried two passengers—Edward Fiddler, a farmer from Prince Albert, and John Betts, a prominent politician. Still scorning a mask, Garnett waved a double-barrelled shotgun at the surprised trio and ordered them from the stage. When they hesitated to obey, he cocked the shotgun. They jumped.

Garnett forced Art and Betts to kneel while he trussed their arms, and under threat of the gun made Fiddler conceal the stage behind a bluff. Safely off the road, Garnett lost little time. "Driver, where is the box?"

"I don't know nothing about a box," John Art replied.

Garnett leaped onto the stage but failed to locate a strongbox. He kicked the mail sacks to the ground, ripped them open and selected the registered letters. John Art shifted his feet in embarrassment. "I feel awful silly letting one man hold us up," he protested.

"You needn't," Garnett assured him. "My partner and I held up a larger party than yours this morning. He's over there behind the bluff covering you now."

Although he searched the three men, he took nothing—not even Betts's $250 in cash. As a final gesture of goodwill, Garnett shared with them a bottle of whisky he had found on the stage.

Having left behind eight men capable of identifying him, Garnett rode back to Salt Springs. Here he retrieved his cart and then drove 160 kilometres to Carrot River, where he sought to establish an alibi by registering a homestead. That done, he returned to his ferry and, in the presence of his substitute ferryman, shaved off his distinctive beard and mustache. The proceeds of the two robberies was $1,465.40. After burying the money in a tin can a short distance from the ferry, Garnett resumed his duties and his accustomed role of respectability.

A month later, business took Garnett to Prince Albert and there retribution overtook him. He was recognized by John Art, the stagecoach driver, and arrested by the NWMP. A preliminary hearing was held before Superintendent Perry, and Garnett was sent to Regina to stand trial.

Perry immediately issued a search warrant to locate the missing money. Though the police tore up Garnett's home, ripped planks from his ferry and prowled the surrounding brush, all they found were several articles of clothing later identified by the victims as those worn by Garnett.

While in Regina prison awaiting trial, Garnett disclosed the location of his cache to a cellmate, Peter Smith, who operated a stagecoach stopping house near Touchwood. When Smith was released early in September, he hired a Metis guide and went straight to the cache. Elated with his new-found wealth, Smith gave the ferryman $5 for use of the ferry and another $5 for a meal. For Smith, however, the money proved fatal.

Apparently of a shrewder nature than Garnett, Smith returned to his shack beside the Prince Albert Trail. Police suspicion focused on him briefly, but as he had outwardly resumed his meagre way of life, interest in him soon waned.

Main Street, Prince Albert, Saskatchewan, where Garnett
was recognized and arrested. GLENBOW ARCHIVES NA-1338-43

The following May, Smith announced his intention of leaving.
When he did disappear, nobody thought much about it.

Some days later, Smith's body was found in the bushes by
a passing freighter. Suspicion centred on a Native boy, Nan-
nan-kase-lex. He had suddenly acquired an unusual amount
of money, and large sums of cash were not part of the way of
life for either Natives or settlers in the 1880s. He was taken to
Regina, charged with the murder of Peter Smith, and examined by Inspector Norman of the NWMP. Nan-nan-kase-lex

said the money had been given to him by a Native woman friend. While no supportive evidence was forthcoming, the investigation revealed the then unknown account of Smith's visit to the Garnett ferry for the hidden money.

Garnett's trial opened on October 7, 1886, before Judge Hugh Richardson. The evidence conclusively tied him to the crimes. Despite the testimony of three character witnesses—including Archdeacon Marsh, who had travelled from Winnipeg at considerable expense—Garnett was sentenced to fourteen years in prison. While the sentence was severe in view of his past record of honesty and industry, Judge Richardson declared that a harsh penalty was necessary to discourage the lawless element from preying upon defenceless stagecoaches.

As Convict 23, Garnett settled into the bleak routine of Stony Mountain Penitentiary, near Winnipeg. Since he had always been closely associated with the church, it was no surprise when he obtained the position of servant to the chaplain. Two years later, however, there was a surprise—Garnett purloined a suit of clothes belonging to the preacher, walked out of the prison, and rode away in the padre's horse and buggy.

As with his stagecoach holdup, Garnett's prison escape was notable for a lack of careful planning. He was soon again safely on the inside. After serving eight years he was pardoned and vanished from the records of Western badmen.

7

Gaddy and Racette

JAMES GADDY, A SLIGHTLY BUILT Metis man from the Crooked Lake Reserve, already had a police record when he teamed up with Moise Racette in the early summer of 1887. In addition to minor scrapes with the law, he had served a five-year sentence at Stony Mountain Penitentiary in Manitoba for horse stealing. He was released early for good behaviour, and went back to the reserve in 1884.

Moise Racette was a strong, muscular man of twenty-six when released from the same penitentiary in April 1887. He returned to his home a little north of Wolseley, Saskatchewan. A month later, however, the pair had made contact and together gravitated to Qu'Appelle. They worked at odd jobs when they felt so inclined but were always short of money.

At Qu'Appelle, they had their photographs taken in the tent studio of Allen Sutherland, a photographer from Winnipeg. This whim was later to have disastrous consequences for the pair.

At the time, however, they were not concerned about the future. They had other problems, the main one being a lack of money to pay for the prints when they were ready. To solve their chronic lack of funds, Gaddy suggested that they obtain arms and go on a horse-stealing expedition. Racette liked the idea, and they worked long enough to earn money for two revolvers.

Their next concern was horses. The pair travelled westward to Moose Jaw and stole two ponies and a black mare. Two nights later, on the return trip to Qu'Appelle, they stole a horse from homesteader Hector McLeish. When he discovered his loss, McLeish, a tall Scot renowned for his strength, enlisted the help of his neighbour, and the two started tracking the thieves. At Qu'Appelle, they were joined by Sergeant Tyffe of the NWMP and several citizens. Splitting up, the posse trailed the stolen horse toward Wolseley. From settlers along the way, they obtained a good description of the horse thieves, and Moise Racette was positively identified.

The posse arrived at Wolseley around 10:30 P.M. on May 30. After a conference with Constable Mathewson of the NWMP, most of the men retired for the night at Pritchard's Hotel. McLeish and Mathewson, however, decided to continue to the Racette home 1.6 kilometres north of Wolseley and stand guard during the night. They were to be joined by the posse the following morning.

Shortly after the pair arrived, Moise Racette left the house to saddle his horse in preparation for further flight. McLeish and Mathewson conferred hastily and decided to capture Racette without assistance. Advancing, the constable placed his hand on Racette's arm and pronounced him under arrest. Racette offered no resistance.

Unaware of the policeman's presence, James Gaddy came out of the house and headed toward the corral. Big Hector McLeish stepped from his hiding place to intercept him. Unfortunately, neither McLeish nor Mathewson noticed a third man slip from the cabin's darkened doorway. His presence went undetected until he suddenly flung himself on the constable's back. Racette joined in the attack, knocking Mathewson's revolver away.

As McLeish moved in to help, Gaddy scooped up the fallen pistol and fired three times, hitting McLeish with each shot. When the melee subsided, Mathewson and the third man (who proved to be Racette's father) carried the fatally wounded McLeish into the cabin. In the meantime, Gaddy and Racette worked out a plan to murder the constable. Racette would take Mathewson with him on the pretence of going to Wolseley for a doctor. At a given signal, he would fling himself to the ground so that Gaddy could shoot the policeman.

The plan would have worked except that in the darkness Gaddy's first shot missed its mark. Mathewson spun off the trail, grappling with Racette as two more shots grazed his uniform. He was soon overpowered by the outlaws, but for some reason their plan to kill the constable was abandoned, and they returned with him to the Racette cabin. There, after warning him not to leave until they had gone, they saddled their stolen horses and rode away. As soon as the sound of their horses faded, Mathewson ran for help. A doctor was quickly at the scene and arranged for McLeish to go to Wolseley, but the big Scot died at 8:40 A.M. in the hotel.

For the next few days, angry armed posses of settlers and police surrounded the Crooked Lake Reserve and searched every corner of it. Gaddy and Racette hid out with various friends and, eluding the cordon, headed south through the Cypress Hills into Montana.

Once across the "Medicine Line," as the Natives called the border, they changed their names. Gaddy worked on a sheep ranch, while Racette joined a semi-nomadic band of Montana Metis. He soon married one of the Metis girls.

Meanwhile, photographer Allen Sutherland had completed his summer tour and returned to Winnipeg. Here, he learned of the murder and saw the descriptions of the wanted men. Struck by the resemblance between the outlaws and the two men who had been unable to pay for their photographs earlier that summer, he contacted

Lieutenant-Governor Dewdney. When the photographs proved to be of Gaddy and Racette, Dewdney puchased a dozen for $5 and sent them to the NWMP. Since the police were reasonably certain that the two outlaws were in northern Montana, they forwarded copies of the photograph to Indian agents, army officers, and sheriffs in the area. Weeks passed without results.

Then, on July 18, Gaddy, Racette, and another man named Leroy were seen near Fort Ellice on the Canadian side of the line. A posse was quickly assembled, but after two days of hard riding they discovered that the three men had separated and effectively covered their trails. There followed another long wait, but on August 12 the photographs again assisted the lawmen. Sheriff Beck of Lewiston, Montana, noticed two men at the army post of Fort McGinnis and was positive that they were Gaddy and Racette. Assisted by W.H. Simons, he surprised and arrested them. Word was sent by telegraph to the NWMP at Regina.

Mathewson, now promoted to corporal, the Crown prosecutor, and a settler from Wolseley went to Fort McGinnis, where they identified both men. By November, Gaddy and Racette were lodged in the NWMP cells at Regina. Sheriff Beck and Simons shared the $500 reward.

At a preliminary hearing the trial date was set for January 10, 1888. However, owing to a defence counsel request for an opinion on James Gaddy's "soundness of mind," the trial was postponed for four weeks to February 6.

Main Street, Qu'Appelle, Saskatchewan, where Gaddy and Racette had their photo taken in 1887. GLENBOW ARCHIVES NA-2294-17

Court was held at Wolseley on that date with Mr. Justice Wetmore presiding. A surprise Crown witness was Peter Gaddy, James's brother, who testified that he had seen the entire episode on the night of the McLeish murder. His testimony, as well as that of numerous other witnesses, clinched the Crown's case. Both were convicted and sentenced to death. From the same cellblock that had housed the famous Louis Riel, Gaddy and Racette were led to the scaffold on June 13, 1888.

A grimly humorous footnote was added in 1894. Photographer Allen Sutherland visited the Crooked Lake Reserve that summer and was attracted to an aged Native man whose face he thought would make an excellent portrait. To his surprise, the man refused to pose. Sutherland later learned that the old man didn't want his picture taken "by the machine that hung Gaddy and Racette."

CHAPTER

8

Death Song from the Poplars

WHEN ALMIGHTY VOICE WAS BORN in 1874, his parents, John Sounding Sky and his wife, Spotted Calf, belonged to a small band of Swampy Cree under the leadership of One Arrow. In turn, One Arrow's band was part of a loose association of Crees under the general guidance of Chief Beardy. They hunted on the plains of what would become the province of Saskatchewan and wintered around Batoche and the small community of Duck Lake on the South Saskatchewan River.

Chief Beardy was a sly, cantankerous old man who delighted in upsetting the dignity of civil servants. Thus, when the majority of Plains Cree gathered at Fort Carlton in August 1876 to sign Treaty 6, which would confine them to reserves, Chief Beardy and his associates sent word that they wanted the treaty makers to come to them. After some bickering, a compromise was reached. On August 28, 1876, Chief Beardy, One Arrow, and nine band councillors agreed to the treaty.

The reserve to which One Arrow and his small band retired was near Batoche on the eastern side of the South Saskatchewan River. Its rich, sandy loam was ideally suited to mixed farming—an undertaking of which the Cree knew nothing and cared less. The area comprised open prairie and "islands" of poplar trees in the miles of short prairie grass. These islands, laced with dense underbrush, were known locally as "bluffs." Here, John Sounding Sky and Spotted Calf settled with their only son, Almighty Voice. His Cree name was Kisse-manitou-wayo, but he appeared on the agency records as Jean Baptiste.

On the whole, the One Arrow band strongly resisted the efforts of the Indian Agent to "civilize" them. By the spring of 1885, the band had shrunk to fewer than two hundred because of starvation and disease. Of the survivors, some twenty were able-bodied men who constantly left the reservation without permission and created a problem for the handful of NWMP members stationed at Fort Carlton and Duck Lake.

When the Riel Rebellion erupted in March 1885, One Arrow and all his warriors joined the uprising. After Riel was defeated, One Arrow was deprived of his chieftainship and sentenced to three years in the penitentiary. From then on, the band was without a chief or councillors.

In 1888, R.S. McKenzie was appointed Indian Agent to Duck Lake. He was a thorough, kindly man with a keen insight into human behaviour. One of his first acts was to appoint a Native man, Sandy Thomas, as his official interpreter. Then he selected big, rough, and ready Louis Marion as farm instructor.

Marion threatened and cajoled the Cree to build more substantial houses, plant small grain crops, vegetable gardens and hay fields, and to send their school-age children to the Indian Industrial School at Qu'Appelle. Even John Sounding Sky—one of the more restless braves—yielded to Marion's blandishments and engaged successfully in mixed farming.

By 1895, the people of One Arrow's reserve were struggling out of a state of semi-starvation. But the price had been drastic. Fewer than one hundred men, thirty women, and fifty-nine children were left, many of them suffering disease and malnutrition. Among the remaining men was young Almighty Voice.

At twenty-one, Almighty Voice was tall and slim with a battle scar on his left cheek that ran from mouth to ear. His small hands and feet, fair complexion, and dark wavy hair made him a great favourite with the ladies. Because of the preponderance of women, Almighty Voice, like several of the braves, unofficially took two or three wives.

Kisse-manitou-wayo (Almighty Voice),
Duck Lake area, Saskatchewan, circa 1892–94.

He acquired his first wife, the daughter of Napaise, when he was eighteen. Then he added Kapahoo's daughter, and in the summer of 1895 wooed and won The Rump's daughter. Then his attention shifted some distance to a thirteen-year-old at the Fort à la Corne reserve.

Louis Marion, who closely watched his charges and promptly reported absentee braves to the NWMP, never worried about Almighty Voice's wanderings. He correctly presumed that the popular young brave was off in quest of romantic adventure. Nevertheless, unlike most of the other Cree in the Duck Lake agency, One Arrow's band remained restless and caused difficulties for Marion and the police.

On October 19, 1895, John Sounding Sky was arrested for illegally acquiring a piece of farm equipment belonging to L. Couture, whose farm adjoined the reservation. Sounding Sky was found guilty of theft and sentenced to six months of hard labour.

The next day, while his father was en route to the prison, Almighty Voice arrived from Fort à la Corne with the thirteen-year-old daughter of a man named Old Dust. Her brother, Young Dust, accompanied them. Almighty Voice installed his fourth intended bride in his mother's home and began to prepare for the wedding feast. His current wife, daughter of The Rump, returned to her father.

The fact that food was scarce did not dampen wedding plans. With Young Dust, Almighty Voice visited friends and invited them to a modest wedding feast that night at

John Sounding Sky's house. While returning home, the pair came upon a cow that had wandered onto the reserve. As part of the farming experiment, Indian Agent McKenzie had purchased a small herd of cows for the One Arrow band, which were pastured on the reserve. In addition, one or two farmers whose property adjoined the reservation also owned cattle. Occasionally, one of the animals disappeared. If it was a settler's cow, the matter was treated with firmness, but if an agency cow was missing the matter was considered less serious. Ironically, the cow encountered by Almighty Voice later proved to be neither. It had strayed several miles from its grazing grounds and no one knew its ownership.

Almighty Voice, however, wasn't concerned about who owned it. With a shot from his .45-75 Winchester he solved the problem of feeding his guests. Thanks to the wandering cow, the wedding feast lasted into the night. News that there was plenty of meat spread quickly through the reserve and uninvited guests began to arrive. Among them was Dubling, brother of Almighty Voice's recently discarded wife. Dubling capped his feast by dropping into Marion's home and informing the farm instructor that Almighty Voice had killed an agency cow. The next day, Marion advised Sergeant Colebrook at the Batoche NWMP detachment and then checked his herd. Not a single cow was missing.

The following day, October 22, was treaty payment time at Duck Lake. As Almighty Voice and Young Dust stepped forward to collect their payments, they were taken into custody by Sergeant Colebrook and turned over to Sergeant Harry Keenan, who was in charge of the Duck Lake Detachment. The prison at Duck Lake was a log shack that had been converted into a guard house by the addition of iron bars to the windows. Inside was a single room with a table and chair near the door. The usual procedure was to allow the prisoners to sleep on the floor while the guard slept in his chair. In the event that a dangerous criminal might be incarcerated, several large iron rings had been embedded in the logs for handcuffs or leg shackles.

During the day, Almighty Voice and Young Dust lounged in the yard, and at night they were placed inside the log shed and given blankets. Night duty—especially guarding two peaceful prisoners like Almighty Voice and Young Dust—was boring to Constable Thomas Alexander Dickson. He dozed or played cards until his watch ended at 2 A.M. After a glance at his sleeping prisoners, he walked over to the nearby barracks to awaken Constable Andrew O'Kelly. Not considering his prisoners dangerous, Dickson did not lock the door.

O'Kelly arrived at the guard house some five minutes after Dickson's departure. Young Dust was still sleeping soundly but Almighty Voice had simply walked through the unlocked door into the night. On learning of the escape, Sergeant Keenan, surmising that Almighty Voice would head for John Sounding Sky's cabin, notified

Sergeant Colin Colebrook at Batoche. Constable Dickson was sent to assist in the re-apprehension of the young Cree.

Although the Mounted Police were treating the affair with routine casualness, Almighty Voice, impelled by some sense of urgency, made his way directly to the South Saskatchewan River near Batoche Crossing. The weather was cold, and ice had formed along both banks of the river. Nevertheless, he swam across and made his way to his father's house.

During the next few days, Sergeant Colebrook and Constable Dickson made several surprise visits to the reservation without catching sight of their escaped prisoner. Colebrook was sure that Almighty Voice was somewhere on the reserve, since his young bride had taken ill after the wedding feast. The continued presence of Young Dust was also reassuring. In the meantime, police scout Francis Dumont wandered around the reserve, on the alert for news.

One night Dumont learned that Almighty Voice had secured a pony and left the reserve. His informant suggested that he might be headed for the James Smith Reservation at Fort à la Corne. Dumont rode to Batoche and told Sergeant Colebrook.

The next morning, Colebrook and Dumont left to trail the escapee. A well-travelled trail led from the ferry at Batoche to a settlement at Kinistino, 48 kilometres to the east. Dumont picked up Almighty Voice's tracks along the trail and followed them for some distance. They indicated that Almighty Voice was walking while his wife rode.

Toward evening they met police scout Joe McKay, better known as "Gentleman Joe," one of the picturesque characters of the West. With his fine white beard he resembled Buffalo Bill of Wild West fame, and in 1885 he had fired the first shot in the Riel Rebellion at Duck Lake. After the rebellion he continued his career as a police scout and was stationed at Prince Albert. He had now been sent to Fort à la Corne to intercept Almighty Voice if he showed up.

Learning from McKay that heavy snow had fallen east of Kinistino, Colebrook exchanged his team and democrat for the scout's horse. Until then the fugitive's trail had led southeastward in the direction of the Touchwood Hills. Just before nightfall, however, Colebrook discovered that Almighty Voice had turned north in the direction of his wife's reservation. He decided to camp on the trail and resume pursuit in the morning.

The morning of October 19, 1895, dawned cool and clear. A week had passed since the casual arrest of Almighty Voice and Young Dust at Duck Lake, but beyond the fact that Sergeant Colebrook and Dumont were tired and cold, nothing had altered the routine approach to apprehending the young Cree. But as Colebrook and Dumont rode along the trail that morning, they were startled by the near crack of a rifle. Over a slight rise they saw a Native pony beside the trail. A young girl squatted beside a small fire, while a short distance away a slender young brave emerged from the trees carrying a dead rabbit.

It was Almighty Voice. Each recognized the other instantly. As Colebrook urged his horse forward, the young Cree dropped the rabbit and reloaded his Winchester. Colebrook continued to move forward. Then Almighty Voice called a warning in Cree. The officer's knowledge of Cree was slight, but Dumont translated that Almighty Voice intended to shoot. Ignoring the warning, Colebrook slipped his hand into his pocket and brought out his service revolver. Holding it in his lap, he lifted his free hand in a sign of friendship and urged his horse forward.

Almighty Voice raised his Winchester and covered the advancing officer. Up to this point, Almighty Voice had been a law-abiding if impetuous young man whose worst crime had been killing a stray cow and walking away from an unattended jail. Once recaptured, his sentence would probably be a few days' work on the woodpile. His adversary, Sergeant Colebrook, was a level-headed police officer familiar with serious situations. He obviously was convinced that the young man would not be foolish enough to shoot.

Almighty Voice shouted again. Dumont, warned by his tone of voice, urged the policeman to stop. It was too late. Almighty Voice sent a heavy .45 calibre slug into Colebrook's chest. Stunned momentarily from the impact, he fell from his horse, the unfired revolver slipping from his fingers.

Dumont, fearing for his own life, wheeled his horse and spurred back along the trail until a rise in the ground hid him from view. Scarcely had the police scout decamped than Almighty Voice approached the fallen officer and scooped up his revolver. A glance told him that Colebrook was unconscious. After hurried consultation with his young bride, he mounted the officer's horse and rode eastward. The girl stoically retrieved the rabbit her husband had shot and started to cook it over the fire.

The first policeman Dumont encountered as he headed from the murder scene was Constable Charles Tennent, on patrol with scout Timothy Meyers. Dumont then continued toward Batoche, while Tennent and Meyers rode to where Sergeant Colebrook lay dead. The girl was still eating the rabbit. Tennent dispatched Meyers to a nearby settler named Harper for a wagon. He took the girl into custody, and the party returned to Harper's with Colebrook's body.

In the meantime, Scout Dumont had reported the grim details to Corporal McKenzie at Batoche. Telegraph messages were sent to Duck Lake and every available man from both detachments immediately saddled up and scoured the countryside for the murderer. From Prince Albert came a special detail commanded by Inspector John B. Allen, better known as "Broncho Jack."

Colebrook's funeral took place in the barracks at Prince Albert on November 2. He was buried in St. Mary's Cemetery in a plot with several police killed in the Riel Rebellion. Mourners included ex-constable Ernest Grundy, now postmaster for the little village of Duck Lake. A close friend of the murdered man, Grundy was to play a tragic role attempting to avenge the death of his friend.

In the following weeks, though rumour spurred frequent patrols through the district, the trail grew cold. Almighty Voice's wife was released in the hope that she might lead the police to him, but she merely returned to John Sounding Sky's cabin on One Arrow's reserve. The only development was that Sergeant Harry Keenan, who was in charge of the Duck Lake Detachment when Almighty Voice escaped, was demoted to constable.

This demotion caused an immediate public reaction, spearheaded by the vitriolic editor of the *Saskatchewan Times* in Prince Albert. Harry Keenan had been one of the first men to join the NWMP when it was formed, enlisting on November 3, 1873. He resigned after nine years of service during which time he rose to sergeant, but re-enlisted the following year and quickly reached his former rank. During the unrest that preceded the 1885 Riel uprising, Keenan had effectively scouted the rebels and gave the first warning that they intended to defy the Canadian government. As a result of the public's defence of Keenan, Commissioner Herchmer reinstated him to his former rank.

In the months that followed, Almighty Voice drifted from band to lonely band of Cree. He appeared sometimes at the James Smith Reservation at Fort à la Corne, at other times with the bands near Nut and Quill Lakes, where he had many relatives. In April 1896, the Canadian government

THE LAW AND THE LAWLESS

offered a reward of $500 for information leading to his capture, but the offer solved nothing.

In the meantime, police officers suspected that Almighty Voice had not fled far from his familiar surroundings. In the spring of 1897, his wife gave birth to a son, Stanislaus. Then in May, David and Napoleon Venne, sons of a Metis farmer who lived east of One Arrow's reserve, noticed three Natives chasing their cattle. They pursued the trio to one of the dense poplar bluffs that dotted the rolling prairie.

One of the apparent cattle thieves met misfortune when his pony stumbled in a gopher hole and threw him. Before he could regain his mount, he was captured by the Venne brothers. He gave his name as Little Salteau and named one of his escaped companions as Dubling. The Vennes became suspicious. Little Salteau refused to divulge the third man's identity. But as they had nothing definite to act upon, they released their prisoner.

The following morning they discovered that one of their cows had been slaughtered during the night. The prime suspects were Little Salteau and his companions. Napoleon Venne rode to the NWMP detachment at Batoche, then under the command of Corporal William Bowridge.

Bowridge also thought that the unnamed Native might well be Almighty Voice, and he rode back to the Venne farm to inspect the cow's carcass. The fact that the bulk of the carcass was intact made him more suspicious, and he went directly to John Sounding Sky's cabin. While there was no sign of Almighty Voice, Bowridge learned that Dubling had traded a horse for a rifle the night before.

During his search of the reservation land, Corporal Bowridge saw two men run into a poplar bluff. He rode toward the bluff with Venne at his side. It proved a dangerous move. As they approached the poplar copse, two rifle shots rang out. The first bullet struck Venne in the shoulder, the second creased his rifle butt. Corporal Bowridge assisted his companion to safety and both men returned to Batoche. Venne identified the man who shot him as Dubling. The second man was probably Almighty Voice.

Within an hour of receiving word of the incident, Inspector Allen at Prince Albert had nine men ready for action. The detail was handed over to Sergeant Charles Raven with orders to proceed to the reservation. Then Inspector Allen left for McDowell to pick up a guide and interpreter.

Early on May 28, the two parties met at the St. Louis de Langevin ferry and set out for the Minichinis Hills, east of One Arrow's reserve, where Venne had been shot. Leaving before the main party of police were ready, Inspector Allen reconnoitered the surrounding area from a hill overlooking the prairie. He noticed a movement in the valley to the east but was unable to determine whether the objects were men or deer. In the meantime, a messenger arrived from Sergeant Raven advising the men had been sighted east of the Venne farm.

Meanwhile, Sergeant Raven's men were combing the countryside on both sides of the trail leading to Touchwood Hills. At one point Constable C.M. McNair reported sighting three objects moving ahead of the posse, and the search was intensified. A few moments later, Constable Andrew O'Kelly—the man who had first discovered Almighty Voice's absence from the Duck Lake jail—confirmed he had seen three Native men disappear into a bluff of poplars about 180 metres ahead.

Without waiting for Allen, Raven called in his outriders and rode forward to the bluff. The stand of trees extended in a north-south direction and was heavily overgrown with underbrush. In places it was difficult to see more than a few metres. As he detailed his men to surround the bluff, Raven saw Inspector Allen and guide William Bruce approaching along the main road from the Venne farm.

Taking Constable William Hume, a crack revolver shot, Raven rode to the north end of the bluff and dismounted. He planned to traverse the woods from north to south, and by keeping an equal distance from each edge of the bluff and from each other, cover the entire area in one sweep. With his carbine, a shell in the breech, Raven started into the bush. To his right, Constable Hume advanced abreast, revolver ready. Sergeant Raven later wrote, "We had gone about 50 yards when I came to a narrow opening in the underbrush and caught a glimpse of two Indians, crouched down, about 20 yards from me. They had rifles and fired at once and disappeared in the brush. I fired in their direction, as did Constable Hume, but without result."

Again the Cree had demonstrated their skill with their rifles. Raven was hit twice in the hip, his leg numb and useless. He was dragged from the underbrush by his comrade. Despite the wound, Raven shouted a warning to the men encircling the bluff to watch out for the fugitives, now crashing toward the south end of the copse. Then Raven collapsed.

The constables stationed at intervals round the bluff could see nothing. Although they heard at least five shots, they could only hold their ground and scan the edge of the woods. Inspector Allen, who arrived as Raven was dragged to open ground, demanded: "Who is running? What was that shooting about?" The wounded Raven weakly answered that he was certain one of the men was Almighty Voice trying to escape from the southern end of the copse.

Drawing his revolver, Allen spurred his horse southward along the edge of the bluff and swung into an opening in the willow scrub. He was suddenly confronted by three Native men intent on gaining the open ground. "Here they are, boys!" Allen shouted.

The same instant, Almighty Voice and his companions fired. A heavy slug shattered Allen's right arm and he thudded to the ground. Almighty Voice jumped from shelter and advanced cautiously. Realizing that he and his companions were trapped, his first thought was to secure the fallen officer's ammunition belt. Later, Inspector Allen recalled the incident: "Pulling myself through the twigs to a small ash stump, I was enabled to come to my feet, only to find myself looking into the barrel of an old pattern .45-75 Winchester. Almighty Voice . . . had me covered. The other two Indians had jumped back to safety."

Constable McNair, who was stationed back from the bluff, fired a long shot at the wanted criminal. A few seconds later, Sergeant Raven, realizing Allen's plight, dragged himself upright and opened fire from long range. Constable Hume disregarded his own safety by rushing headlong to the inspector's assistance, firing rapidly from his service revolver. Almighty Voice ignored the ammunition belt and scrambled into the underbrush.

Corporal C. Hockin and Constable J.R. Kerr heard the fusillade from their posts on the west side of the bluff and spurred their horses to where Allen had been ambushed. They opened fire at the spot where the three men had last been seen. Hume had meanwhile reached the unconscious Inspector Allen. Ignoring the desultory sniping from the fugitives, the constable hoisted Allen onto his horse and carried him to safety.

Despite severe wounds, Sergeant Raven returned to the task of repositioning his men round the bluff, hoping to prevent the three men from escaping. Then Inspector Allen recovered consciousness and sent Constable O'Kelly to Batoche to alert the rest of the detachments and to bring medical aid. A short time later, Allen was placed onto a wagon and driven toward Prince Albert.

Almighty Voice, Dubling, and Little Salteau, surrounded by grim-faced policemen, celebrated their first victory with an impromptu war dance, their shouting plainly audible to the men. After a few random shots were pumped into the woods, the war cries ceased. Silence hung over the woods.

At noon, a tentative attempt was made to set fire to the woods, but the grass and trees were too green to ignite. In the late afternoon, an impromptu posse comprising Dr. Stewart from the Indian Agency, Constable A. O'Kelly, and five civilians arrived from Batoche and Duck Lake. One of the civilians was postmaster Ernest Grundy, the ex-constable and close friend of the slain Sergeant Colebrook. The wounded Sergeant Raven was immediately taken to Duck Lake in a buckboard, and Corporal Hockin took charge.

As evening approached, Corporal Hockin faced a difficult decision. A cloudy sky suggested that the night would be dark, affording ample opportunity for Almighty Voice and his companions to slip through the cordon of police and volunteers. He conferred with Constable O'Kelly and the civilians and decided to search the bluff rather than risk losing the three men in the darkness. All concerned had no illusions about the risks, but none could imagine the disaster soon to take place.

To add to the difficulties of those besieging the bluff,

Cree from the One Arrow Reserve began to arrive. Keeping a respectful distance, they made camp on a low hill overlooking the scene. Spotted Calf, Almighty Voice's mother, was among them.

Corporal Hockin suspected that Almighty Voice and his friends might have worked their way toward the north end of the bluff where Raven and Hume had first encountered them. As a consequence he stationed the civilians at vantage points but concentrated them along the southern edge. Then at the head of nine men, he walked to the north end of the woods.

Instead of working his way southward, as did Raven and Hume, the corporal decided to traverse the bluff in an east-west direction. He stationed his men in a line, almost shoulder to shoulder. Forcing through the thick underbrush, the ten men worked their way slowly from one side of the bluff to the other. Without a shot being fired, they emerged on the west side.

They traversed the woods a second time, expecting every moment to be confronted by the crack of rifles. When they emerged on the east side facing the road, they were met by Corporal Bowridge, who took his place in the line as they wheeled for the third approach. As Corporal Hockin moved his men closer to the south end of the bluff he felt the tension mount. He knew it was impossible for the fugitives to have escaped. They had to be in the woods. He also knew that they were deadly shots.

Hockin gave the command and the line moved slowly forward. Faces were stern and fingers closed tensely over revolver butts. Step by step the line worked through the willow underbrush. It reached the halfway point with no sign of the concealed desperadoes. Centering the line—Ernest Grundy on one side, Constable Kerr on the other—Hockin pushed forward. They were almost to the west side of the woods when a burst of gunfire crashed out with startling bitterness.

Grundy dropped, shot through the stomach. Corporal Hockin staggered, a bullet in his chest. On either side of the fatally wounded men, posse members flung themselves down to escape a second fusillade. Desperately they searched the impenetrable screen of grass and willow to locate the ambush. All was silent. After their deadly volley, Almighty Voice and his companions patiently awaited their pursuers' next move.

It was Constable Kerr who detected a slight movement in the underbrush. Signalling to O'Kelly, Kerr pointed and indicated that he was going to charge. O'Kelly nodded his readiness. Simultaneously, the two policemen leaped to their feet and ran toward a low pile of logs. They had scarcely moved before a volley shattered the silent woods and Kerr slumped forward, a bullet through his heart. Constable O'Kelly dropped to the ground and worked his way back to the wounded Corporal Hockin. Nearby members of the search party opened fire on the logs, but a steady return fire warned them not to expose their position.

The command to retire was given. With painstaking

care the remaining men worked their way back through the underbrush—feet first and heads in the direction of the ambush. With assistance, O'Kelly dragged the inert Hockin with him. No attempt was made to rescue Kerr, whose body was in full view of the concealed rifle pit. Postmaster Grundy had died and he, too, had to be left.

As the posse emerged from the bluff, farm instructor Marion, who had been vainly trying to persuade the watching Natives to return to the reserve, leaped into his wagon and raced toward the woods. The wounded corporal was drawn to the safety of the road. Even as he was being placed in the wagon, a long-range shot from the bluff caught a civilian in the heel. Although Dr. Stewart rendered immediate attention, Hockin's wound proved fatal and he died on the way to the hospital at Duck Lake.

As darkness fell over the Minichinis Hills, the police kept an all-night vigil by the light of huge bonfires circling the bluff. The incident that had begun with a wandering cow of no known origin had now claimed four lives. Those watching the bluff couldn't help wondering who would be next.

The Death Song

At Prince Albert, telegraphic dispatches told of mounting casualties and that the Cree from One Arrow Reserve were moving slowly to the scene of the fighting. Fearing another uprising, Superintendent Severe Gagnon organized members of the Prince Albert Volunteers, a militia group that had seen active service during the Riel Rebellion.

From detailed reports, Gagnon realized that the three fugitives were in an advantageous position, and he resolved to treat the matter as a military campaign. Readying the brass seven-pounder cannon at the detachment, he loaded a wagon with shells and prepared to set off. Then it was discovered that no one in the force knew how to fire the cannon. Further delay ensued while a civilian was commandeered to operate it.

Late in the night, with eight policemen and volunteers— among them Surgeon Bain and Hospital Sergeant West—Gagnon left Prince Albert. On Saturday morning, May 29, the group reached the ferry over the South Saskatchewan River at McKenzie Crossing. Here Gagnon met the wounded Inspector Allen. As Surgeon Bain dressed the policeman's shattered arm, Gagnon learned of the problems confronting the police and civilians at the bluff. After an early breakfast he led the little column southward toward the poplar bluff and its murderous occupants.

Meanwhile, Commissioner Herchmer of Regina had been kept informed by telegraph. On Friday morning he learned of the wounding of Inspector Allan and Sergeant Raven and decided to send ten more policemen to the area. That night, however, during a ball in honour of a police contingent leaving to participate in Queen Victoria's Diamond Jubilee celebrations, Herchmer received more ominous news. *The Leader* at Regina reported:

Just before midnight, and while a waltz was in progress, Commissioner Herchmer got the message of the killing of Corp. Hockin, Const. Kerr and Mr. Grundy. Suddenly the music ceased and the reason of its cessation passed quickly around. The dance was ended. Upon further information received during the night, the Commissioner decided to send out a larger force than was first intended. The bustle of loading a field piece, and horses, and the sending of so considerable a force as twenty-five men, with the Asst. Commissioner, aroused no little excitement. The regular train being unable to exceed schedule time, a special was chartered. It may be noted that it was just 30 minutes after C.P.R. Agent Birbeck was given the order for a special train, that it left the depot towards the scene of action.

With the policemen went a correspondent from *The Leader*, who wrote the following account:

The last sound from friends that greeted the Regina detachment of the N.W.M.P. as they left to capture Almighty Voice was the ringing cheer of the citizens as the train drew out of the depot. The men were pleased with this recognition and it made them more determined than ever that, so far as they were concerned, Almighty Voice was doomed—to be either caught or killed. This was at half-past ten on Saturday morning, and by 4:50 p.m. we were at Duck Lake station, after the fastest run ever made on the Prince Albert branch . . . The force then set off to Batoche, crossed One Arrow's reserve and passed through the Belle Vue settlement to Minetchinase [Minichinis], or "the beautiful bare hills" amid which Almighty Voice had been driven to bay . . .

128

Death Song from the Poplars

While driving through the reserve we passed the home of Almighty Voice. His wife was standing on the threshold. She made a motion as we passed: but whether it was intended to express encouragement, derision or contempt it was too dark to see, but from the temper shown all along it was likely a gesture of defiance. It was eleven o'clock at night when the last of the four equipage rigs arrived at the camp. It was very dark and a slight mist hung over the ground. It was a night most favourable for crawling out of a bluff, and this made the sentries all the more determined to keep alert. The men from Prince Albert, Duck Lake and Batoche were at their third night's watch, having had but the roughest of food snatched at intervals, and so little rest that not a kit had been unrolled. The cordon round the bluff was strengthened by the Regina men, and it was felt that the outlaw was so hemmed in that escape was impossible. The mother of Almighty Voice visited the camp. She said: 'There are many of you and you may catch him and kill him, but he will kill many of you first . . .

The Indian "Doubling" (also spelled Dubling) came to the edge of the bluff and shouted something in Cree. What he said is not exactly known. One person translated it as a defiant message thus: "You have fired long but you will have to do better than that." Another says that what Doubling said was: "You have fired long, now send us something to eat," which, as after events showed, is much more probable.

The night was a night of watching, cold and dark. A few of us who were not watching stood round a camp fire longing for the dawn and what it would bring forth. The monotony was relieved by an occasional perambulation of the pickets and the only sound heard was the frequent click of a carbine as a sentry, or more than one, fired at one or other of the occupants of the bluff. On one occasion sentries fired at opposite ends of the bluff at the same time, and it is pretty certain that the two Indians were simultaneously endeavoring to leave the bluff in opposite directions . . .

Once a bullet came whizzing amongst us who were standing round the fire, a visitor that certainly was not particularly welcome. At the first faint streak of dawn there was a lively rattle from the Winchesters all round the bluff, as though in the dim light the whole cordon imagined they saw the enemy.

The time had now arrived for preparing for the day's work. The horses were taken to the nearest water, a mile away. Ultimately the team was fixed to the nine-pounder and it was drawn to a position covering the corner of the bluff opposite to where the seven-pounder was pointed. Precisely at six o'clock both cannons opened fire . . . Smith guided the nine-pounder with deadly aim, and Walton did destructive work with the seven-pounder that had distinguished itself at the Duck Lake fight in 1885. For an hour a perfect shower of shrapnel and grape was poured into the bluff. The shells were timed to burst with admirable precision at 700 yards and it is difficult to imagine that any portion of the bluff escaped the deadly missiles. Neither of the Indians gave any sign of their appreciation of these attentions. The nine-pounder was christened "Almighty Voice" . . .

At ten o'clock the firing ceased, and all was silence . . . *The Leader* representative preached the doctrine that the men were either dead or had escaped, because the habitual wail to the gods had not been heard that morning, and this is a point savages never neglect. Subsequent events showed that his assumption was not far astray. After a short time people showed signs of weariness at waiting, and a rush on the bluff was talked of. Asst.-Com. McIlree, however, did not think the time had arrived for that, consistent with the orders he had received. The orders before leaving Regina were that he was not to rush the bluff until he was satisfied that all had been done with the guns that could be done, as it was useless to risk any lives when it was certain that the outlaws could not escape, and it was cheaper to pay for special trains than to risk lives . . . The Asst.-Commissioner decided on another plan. He decided to dig out the culprits. Messengers were despatched to Duck Lake and Prince Albert to get shovels, mattocks and grub hoes. With these, trenches or ditches were to be dug so that the attackers, under cover, could get right up to where the men were hiding.

Before the implements to do this arrived, however, the patience of the Volunteers was exhausted, and they determined to storm the bluff . . . McIlree was consulted and explained his orders. The men, however, kept to their determination, and there was nothing left for it but for the police to take the lead in the dash. A splendid rush was made, accompanied by a vigorous fusillade. Asst.-Com. McIlree, Insp. Macdonnell, and Insp. Wilson led the police with a gallant dash. Wm. Drain (one of Riel's capturers), Thos. McKay, Timber-Agent Cook, and others led on the Volunteers of Prince Albert and Batoche, Jas. McKay, Q.C., cheering them on from his horse as he rode by the side of the bluff. It was a brave rush and loses nothing of its gallant quality from the fact that it was unnecessary. The Indians were all dead and the bodies cold. Dr. Bain said they had been dead several hours. Had they been alive it is improbable from the vantage position they had that they could have been captured without the loss of half a dozen men, if not more. Both Indians, Almighty Voice and his youthful companion, had been shelled to death in the very refuge they had so patiently dug for their security. The Voice's skull had been shattered by a piece of exploded shell. Doubling's body was found at a short distance ... he was dressed in Kerr's uniform and wore his ring. Perhaps, too, poor and brave Kerr had not died immediately from the shot in his lungs, for a bullet had been put through his head and his skull battered in with his own carbine, portions of hair, blood and brain having clung to the lock. Insp. Macdonnell took charge of the Winchester. Perhaps, however, the mutilation was after death.

The rest is soon told. The Indians were buried on the spot. The bodies of Kerr and Grundy were respectfully taken to Duck Lake to await burial.

Thus ended the eyewitness account of the newspaper reporter. A thorough search of the bluff failed to locate the presence of any other Natives. Later, Thomas McKay discovered a trail of blood where Almighty Voice had dragged himself ninety metres across the open prairie during the night, only to be turned back by the sentries.

By mid-afternoon, the clearing around the deadly little patch of poplar trees was deserted. The tragic sequence of events that began with Almighty Voice killing a cow of unknown ownership had ended.

Selected Bibliography

Books

Anderson, Frank W. *Hanging in Canada: A Concise History of a Controversial Topic.* Surrey, BC: Heritage House Publishing, 1973.

Denny, Cecil E. *Denny's Trek: A Mountie's Memoir of the March West.* Victoria, BC: Heritage House Publishing, 2004.

Higginbotham, J.D. *When the West Was Young: Historical Reminiscences of the Early Canadian West.* Toronto: Ryerson Press, 1933.

Russell, Charles M. *Good Medicine: Memories of the Real West.* Garden City, NY: Garden City Publishing Company, 1930.

Steele, Samuel B. *Forty Years in Canada: Reminiscences of the Great North-West, with Some Account of His Service in South Africa.* Toronto: McClelland & Stewart, 1914.

Newspapers and Magazines

The Calgary Herald, Mining and Ranche Advocate and General Advertiser

Canadian Illustrated News

Macleod Gazette

Manitoba Daily Free Press

The Regina Leader

Royal Canadian Mounted Police Quarterly

Winnipeg Manitoban

List of Authors

Index

Index

139

About the Editor

Art Downs (1924–96) was a writer, editor, historian, and pioneer of BC book and magazine publishing. Born in England, he moved to Saskatchewan as a young child and later settled in Quesnel, BC. He became owner of the *Cariboo Digest*, which evolved into *BC Outdoors*, a successful magazine about BC history, wildlife, and conservation. In 1979, Art and his wife, Doris, established the company that would become Heritage House Publishing. He died in Surrey, BC, in 1996.

More Great Amazing Stories

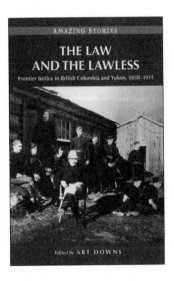

The Law and the Lawless

Frontier Justice in British Columbia and Yukon, 1858–1911

Edited by Art Downs

print ISBN 978-1-927527-89-4
ebook ISBN 978-1-927527-90-9

Gold rush fever in the 1860s brought thousands of miners to the new territories of British Columbia and Yukon armed with rifles, revolvers, and bowie knives. Within months, a provincial police force was recruited to preserve order in the colonies. From Boone Helm, the West's most vicious criminal, to the Wild McLean Gang, who terrorized the Okanagan and Nicola Valley, to Yukon's "Christmas Day assassins," these stories bring to life the early days of policing in the West.

Visit heritagehouse.ca to see the full list of Amazing Stories titles.

More Great Amazing Stories

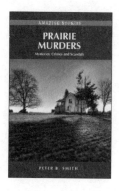

Prairie Murders
Mysteries, Crimes and Scoundrels

Peter B. Smith

print ISBN 978-1-894974-71-4
ebook ISBN 978-1-926936-26-0

From a deadly Prohibition-era shootout to a landmark case solved with DNA evidence, these are riveting stories of Prairie murderers and the people who fought to bring them to justice.

CSI Alberta
The Secrets of Skulls and Skeletons

Peter B. Smith

print ISBN 978-1-894974-84-4
ebook ISBN 978-1-926936-16-1

These baffling Alberta cases show how dogged, old-fashioned detective work combines with modern forensic techniques in the search for the truth.

Visit heritagehouse.ca to see the full list of Amazing Stories titles.

More Great Amazing Stories

Dirty Thirties Desperadoes

Forgotten Victims of the Great Depression

Rich Mole

print ISBN 978-1-926613-95-6
ebook ISBN 978-1-926936-64-2

In 1935, three Doukhobor farm boys embarked on a violent trail of robbery and murder from Manitoba to Alberta. By the time the spree ended, seven people would be dead.

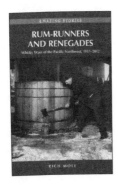

Rum Runners and Renegades

Whisky Wars of the Pacific Northwest, 1917–2012

Rich Mole

print ISBN 978-1-894974-71-4
ebook ISBN 978-1-926936-26-0

From vicious marine hijackers to bedeviled police to corrupt politicians on both sides of the border, this is an action-filled account of liquor and lawlessness on the West Coast.

Visit heritagehouse.ca to see the full list of Amazing Stories titles.

More Great Amazing Stories

Lost Lemon Mine
Unsolved Mysteries of the Old West

Ron Stewart

print ISBN 978-1-926613-99-4
ebook ISBN 978-1-926936-66-6

The Lemon Mine story remains one of the most enduring unsolved mysteries of the Canadian West; despite exhaustive searches by treasure seekers and historians, the mine has never been located.

Whisky Wars of the Canadian West
Fifty Years of Battles Against the Bottle

Rich Mole

print ISBN 978-1-926613-93-2
ebook ISBN 978-1-926936-99-4

A turbulent history of alcohol, Prohibition, and temperance movements resulting from the West's insatiable thirst for liquor.

Visit heritagehouse.ca to see the full list of Amazing Stories titles.